# Conversations with
# Harold H. Saunders

# Conversations with
# Harold H. Saunders
## U.S. Policy for the
## Middle East in the 1980s

American Enterprise Institute for Public Policy Research
Washington and London

**Library of Congress Cataloging in Publication Data**

Saunders, Harold H.
 Conversations with Harold H. Saunders.

 (AEI studies ; 346)
 1. Near East—Foreign relations—United States.
 2. United States—Foreign relations—Near East.
 I. American Enterprise Institute for Public Policy
 Research. II. Title. III. Series.
 DS63.2.U5S28     327.73056     81–20479
 ISBN 0–8447–3473–X             AACR2

AEI Studies 346

*Printed in the United States of America*

# Contents

# Introduction

JUDITH KIPPER

*American Enterprise Institute*

The Middle East, a region historically plagued by violence and unpredictability, has again been plunged into uncertainty by current events. These events have heightened a dangerous rivalry between the United States and the Soviet Union in what some consider the strategic center of the world. The region's balance of power has shifted. Strategic alliances, regional economic cooperation, and steady supplies of oil are directly involved in the changing conditions in the Middle East, where more U.S. interests come together than in any other area. The stakes in this vital region have probably never been higher.

As the Reagan administration continues the process of fashioning policy for the Middle East, the intricate interrelationship of the strategic problems in the region calls for an analysis of the conditions necessary for stability, peace, and security. The American Enterprise Institute was privileged to have Harold Saunders give his analyses in a series of four conversations in June and July 1981. As assistant secretary of state for Near Eastern and South Asian affairs from 1978 to 1981, Saunders helped make policy during a critical period in the history of the region. He was a member of the negotiating team that produced five Arab-Israeli agreements. He has served as director of intelligence and research at the State Department and was a member of the National Security Council staff from 1961 to 1974.

The first conversation concentrates on America's long-term interests in the Middle East, which include Israel and the Arab countries, the Persian Gulf, Iran, Afghanistan, Pakistan, and the Indian Ocean. In this area, Saunders reviews America's vital interests:

- ensuring the independence, stability, and political orientation of the key states in the area
- preventing Soviet predominance
- safeguarding the security and prosperity of Israel

1

- maintaining the steady flow of oil and Arab economic power
- balancing the buildup of advanced technology weapons, including nuclear weapons
- supporting principles essential to strengthening world order.

The second conversation focuses on the constraints and opportunities for U.S. foreign policy in the Middle East. Forces of change—social, economic, political, and strategic—can produce instability in this vital region. These forces are often unpredictable and beyond anyone's control resulting in reactions that may sometimes substitute for policy.

In our first meeting, Harold Saunders reminded us that geographically the Middle East and Southwestern Asia include Israel and the Arab countries, the Persian Gulf, Iran, Afghanistan, Pakistan, and the Indian Ocean. "Power," Harold Saunders says, "is the ability to change the course of events."

The third conversation with Harold Saunders focuses on a topic that constantly requires redefinition in the Middle East: the Soviet threat, what it is, and what it is not. Early in this administration, it was declared that the highest priority in the Middle East would be "to arrest the deteriorating position of the West vis-à-vis the Soviet Union." Some believe that the Soviet threat in the Middle East makes local issues of secondary importance. An American military presence in the region would be a signal to the Soviets to avoid reckless moves, according to the White House. U.S. troops as part of the Sinai peacekeeping force may be the beginning of a long-term U.S. military presence in the area. The strategic consensus that the administration hopes to create among moderate states, including Egypt, Israel, Pakistan, Turkey, and Saudi Arabia, is designed to prevent Soviet inroads in the region, to protect vital oil supplies, and to check Soviet adventurism. A key to this policy is increased arms sales in the region.

Others believe that the way to keep the Soviets out of the Middle East is to resolve the Palestinian problem. The Palestinian issue, the core of the Middle East conflict, requires a political solution that most in the region claim would pave the way for the strategic consensus the U.S. seeks. Unresolved, the Palestinian issue strains U.S. relations with many friendly nations, threatens Israeli-Egyptian relations, and increases the risk of instability in a region undergoing rapid political, social, and economic change. The Soviet Union can be expected to take advantage of these factors to strengthen its influence in the Middle East.

The United States has considerable strategic and political assets in the region to fashion a policy that will safeguard U.S. interests there. Harold Saunders discusses some of the key factors in fashioning such a policy.

In the last conversation of the series Harold Saunders discusses the Arab-Israeli peace process. Supplying the missing ingredients to make the negotiations between Israel and its neighbors significant may now seem to be more remote than ever. The armed conflict that has broken out between the Israelis and the Palestinians, however, dramatically underscores the urgency of supplying those ingredients to make it possible for the parties to enter into negotiations. To whom does this difficult task fall?

The United States more than ever has a unique role to play as mediator. In seeking peace, the parties to the conflict, both Arab and Israeli, have always turned to the United States. American efforts to effect a cease-fire have been supported by the Israeli cabinet. One of the problems, of course, is that the United States does not have contact with one of the parties to the conflict.

The constant turmoil in the Middle East has occurred at a time when the Reagan administration is attempting to fashion a policy for the region. U.S. mediation in the area could potentially be more effective if American policy were outlined in broad terms for our own people as well as for the parties to the conflict. The extreme sensitivity of the issues requires a direct confrontation with the fundamental problems, which can no longer be avoided. Polarization and an escalating cycle of violence are inherent dangers in the process of getting the parties to the negotiating table. Contradictory claims of each side could lead to greater intransigence when conciliation is required. The complexities and difficulties of launching a new round of negotiations that would include all the parties is a major challenge for the administration.

A global consensus has emerged that the Arab-Israeli conflict requires a political solution. Progress toward satisfying the minimum requirements of Israel and the Palestinians appears to be an essential element in such a solution.

The need for a historical compromise by Israelis and Palestinians is made more intractable by the lack of empathy between them. Terrorism is a function of nonsettlement. Both the Israelis and the Palestinians have a deep need to take care of themselves and to remain independent. Fear and frustration on both sides often lead to violence, destruction, and diminished belief in the promise of diplomacy.

There can be no doubt that resolution of the Arab-Israeli conflict will be reached only by the parties themselves, but getting the parties to the negotiating table has become an American obligation. U.S.

support of Israel will remain a strong, permanent commitment. The United States will also have to evaluate its own vital interests in the region and to pursue a Mideast policy accordingly. The reconciliation of these sometimes contradictory elements poses perhaps the greatest challenge for the United States.

The United States needs to encourage a tendency toward co-existence in the Middle East to break the vicious circle of violence that disrupts movement toward a negotiated settlement. It is important to begin by negating the factors that are a threat to each side. Perpetuation of the current situation presents grave dangers and is intolerable in human terms for the parties.

# 1

# Toward a National Consensus

A CONVERSATION WITH HAROLD H. SAUNDERS

*June 8, 1981*

I start with the proposition that the U.S. role as a world power in the 1990s and beyond will be shaped heavily by the way we handle the Middle East problem in the 1980s. America's global position will be tested more severely in the Middle East and Southwest Asia than it was in Vietnam, because much more is at stake there.

The Middle East and Southwest Asia will dominate the world stage for Americans in the 1980s as Europe did in the 1940s, as Northeast Asia did in the 1950s, and as Southeast Asia did in the 1960s. I am not saying we will have half a million troops in this area by 1990; but the area will claim as high a level of national attention, will engage a broader range of American interests and emotions, and will have an even greater capacity to divide us.

In stating this proposition so starkly, I intend in no way to diminish the continuing critical importance of our relations with the other superpowers and with our allies. I acknowledge the significance of other potentially profound changes, such as those that may now be underway in Eastern Europe. This area, however, will be center stage as it provides repeated shocks to major interests, as it requires the continuing engagement of our highest officials, and as it has the potential to affect our daily lives and the capacity to provoke nationwide controversy.

This is neither an idle nor a parochial statement. It is the starting point I suggest for a statement of priority. The question it leads to is this: What priority in the scale of national interests should we assign to the involvement of our government in efforts to minimize or resolve conflict in the Middle East and Southwest Asia?

Answering this question is the first step in forming a national consensus on these issues. Without a clear and consistent political mandate, it will not be possible to conduct a coherent policy toward this complex area in the 1980s.

5

## American Interests in the 1980s

My proposition about the importance of the Middle East in the 1980s may or may not seem overly dramatic. A judgment on that must take account of the fact that more globally vital issues, and more important U.S. interests, come together in this area than in any other part of the developing world today.

Two points strike me as I review these interests. First, the list of American interests in this area has remained relatively constant over the last two decades, but the way we perceive these interests and talk about them changed dramatically in the mid-1970s. It is still changing. The challenge to our interests will become greater, not less.

Furthermore, unlike the situation in the 1970s, *all* of our interests today are under active, simultaneous challenge. This creates a problem for the policy maker more serious than we may have recognized.

Noting very quickly what could happen to each of these interests in the near 1980s will give us a way to look quickly at the dynamic area we are talking about and the dangers it poses for us. It will give me a chance to describe what I have begun calling the "five faces of the Middle East problem"—the five complexes of interests and issues that compose what we call the Middle East problem as the United States will have to deal with it in this decade.

Our *first* interest is the independence, stability, and political orientation of the key states in the area. Their independence is important because of our interest in seeing these states in a critical area remain free of Soviet domination. Their stability and political orientation are important because of the difficulty of pursuing the full range of our interests in unstable or hostile conditions.

The rapid pace of economic, technological, social, and political change brings with it the threat of instability, which can profoundly alter the character of a nation and its orientation among the superpowers. It can jeopardize independence by inviting the involvement of the superpowers.

The pace of change in this area has accelerated sharply since the mid-1970s. Rarely has such a variety of developments hit one region in less than one generation. That acceleration will continue. The revolution in Iran dramatized the way in which the position of the United States, the global strategic balance, and the economic health of poor and industrialized nations alike can be threatened by explosive internal change and superpower reaction to it.

There is also revolutionary change of a different kind in the evolving peace process between Israel, the Arab states, and the Palestinian movement. If the peace and normalization of relations could be expanded, the door to new opportunities for regional order would be opened.

Our *second* complex of interests can be stated this way: We have long recognized the strategic importance of preventing Soviet predominance in this area and of avoiding the confrontation that would result from a Soviet effort to achieve predominance there. In the 1980s, apart from the independent development of American and Soviet military power and barring a major reorientation in Eastern Europe, this volatile area could well be the principal arena for shaping the global balance of power in the 1990s.

The lines between East and West have been clearly drawn by precedent and by practice in Europe and Northeast Asia, less clearly in Southeast Asia. There are no lines in the Middle East and Southwest Asia, and Soviet expansionism threatens the free world's lifeblood there in a way that we have not experienced in more than three decades. This occurs just at a time when the energy crunch is moving toward its peak.

Against that background, a new security system will have to emerge in this central area. That new system will require both the strengthening of the key countries in the area to resist external attack and internal subversion and a relationship between the United States and the Soviet Union that avoids confrontation while blocking further Soviet aggression. It will also require clarity about the readiness of the United States to support the independence of these nations, and one of the most difficult issues we face is to define exactly what our security position and relationships should be.

Our *third* interest is in assuring the security and prosperity of Israel. The future of Israel and perhaps even of the Jewish people is at stake.

The United States has long had a firm commitment to the security of Israel. That commitment, itself undiminished, has taken on new dimensions. Israel's military setbacks in the first days of the 1973 war caused Israel itself to feel new fear and respect for growing Arab military strength. The oil embargo of 1973–1974 demonstrated how the growing economic power of the Arab states could also be used in ways that would jeopardize global economic stability and drive sharp wedges between the United States and its closest allies. With the military option less viable since the Egyptian-Israeli peace treaty, use of the oil weapon may be more likely in time.

With all of these increased dangers, Egyptian President Anwar Sadat's trip to Jerusalem and the Egyptian-Israeli peace treaty demonstrate that a fundamental shift in Arab attitudes has begun, that progress has been made in gaining acceptance for Israel, and that peace is possible. At the same time, the Palestinian liberation movement has won recognition of most of the members of the United Nations, including our European allies. In the developing world, the Palestinians have become a symbol of many of the injustices it feels it has suffered at the hands of the industrialized world. We can expect mounting pressures from new quarters against Western interests on behalf of the Palestinians.

We must be careful to say that neither a Palestinian settlement nor an Arab-Israeli peace will assure stability in the Middle East. Instability within the Arab states and conflicts among them will continue. Nevertheless, it is also true that a total deadlock on the Palestinian problem and utter lack of hope for these 4 million people who call themselves Palestinians will virtually assure perpetuation of the war against Israel. A continuing deadlock may gradually force moderate governments into the rejectionist camp out of desperation, thereby influencing the political shape of the Middle East for the remainder of this century. It could produce a confrontation between the United States and its allies and leave the United States isolated from them, from the Soviet Union, and from much of the developing world.

Our *fourth* interest relates to the steady flow of oil and to Arab economic power derived from substantial financial reserves. The ever-growing need for a steady supply of vital oil has made this area a tempting target for Soviet aggression. In addition, the way in which the oil-producing states of the Middle East use their oil and money will have profound economic and political consequences both for the United States and global economic stability and for the lives of hundreds of millions of people around the world, in the industrialized and developing nations alike.

The coming decade may be the period in which the global supply-demand equation is under the greatest pressure. Although projections on this subject are constantly being discussed, it seems reasonable to say that the overall production of oil is unlikely to increase as much in the 1980s as overall demand for energy. The 1980s will also be a period when shocks external to the supply-demand system are highly likely. We have already experienced the consequences of the 1973 Arab-Israeli war, the Iranian revolution, and the Iranian-Iraqi war, and the possibility for further unexpected shocks is extensive.

The oil of the Middle East and the revenues derived from its sale at high prices have thrust the oil-producing nations of that area into a world position that they did not design for themselves. In

8

addition to the questions of global energy supply, the problem of stabilizing the economies of nations in heavy debt from financing oil imports is one of the critical issues facing the world today. The possession of surplus revenues in large amounts puts the oil-producing governments squarely in the middle of a wide spectrum of North-South issues.

Our *fifth* interest is the newest comer to a prominent place on our list of interests in its own right: We have long had an interest in preventing an arms imbalance that would make war more likely, but in this decade we will have to face a collection of problems surrounding the buildup of advanced technology weapons, including nuclear weapons.

The United States has since the 1960s been a significant supplier of conventional arms to moderate nations in the Middle East. Through the same period, the United States has worked against the proliferation of nuclear weapons into this area and has urged its industrialized allies to join in this effort. But the manufacture of conventional arms in the area and the development of nuclear devices are advancing.

On the one hand, it is difficult to deny nations of the region access to reasonable supplies of advanced weapons necessary to their own defense. It is unrealistic to think of formal arms limitation without peace—Arab-Israeli peace, reduction of tension among Arabs, some limitation of the Soviet threat, and restraint by all suppliers of arms. On the other hand, there are compelling arguments for looking toward some effort at arms limitation, especially in the nuclear area.

There is one other set of U.S. interests that requires special mention. It is not peculiar to the Middle East. It may be argued that it should not even be considered as part of the calculus of national interest. But it is increasingly a factor in determining the American position in the Middle East.

There will be no argument that credibility is a critical element of American power, but there will be argument when someone asks, Credibility about what? One school will reply that it is important that adversaries see U.S. military power as a believable threat and that friends believe we will use it in their support. There has been much talk about restoring credibility in this area. Another school asks what America stands for in the world. Does it support principles such as freedom from discrimination on grounds of religion or ethnic background? Such as self-determination? Such as the inadmissibility of the acquisition of territory by war? In the eyes of many, both in the industrialized and in the developing worlds today, American credibility in this area is in grave jeopardy.

We have had a long debate in this country about the role of principle in American foreign policy. The time has come, in a world where power is increasingly diffused, to see both military might and principle as critical elements of American power.

## A Policy for Pursuing These Interests

If this analysis of our interests leads to the conclusion that an active U.S. policy in this area is justified, the next question is to devise a policy approach, a strategy for pursuing these interests. Let me underscore at the outset those words, *policy approach*. We cannot here in a short time do the secretary of state's job for him and devise detailed policy to pursue each of the main interests I have outlined.

The questions here today are fundamental ones: How do we approach an area where our interests are as complex, and sometimes conflicting, as they are in the Middle East and Southwest Asia? How do we order our priorities within an area like this? These are not just abstract questions. The answers, in the end, can govern action in the most concrete ways. The answers can generate heated public debate, sometimes over unspoken issues.

Today in the United States there is no consensus. There is not even a common view of what the main problems are.

The policy maker's job begins with analysis of what the issues are, an analysis of exactly what the problem is. This in itself can become the subject of intense public and policy debate. Think of how many answers we have heard to the implied question, What are the key issues for the United States in the Middle East? The following are just a few of many answers—not mine, but a collection from the current market of ideas.

1. Our credibility and strength depend on showing friendly re- gimes we will stand by them and not let them down as we let the shah down or as we have let our friends in Lebanon down.

*Or:* Our credibility depends on our standing up for those who seek social justice, human rights, release from the grip of poverty, and political self-determination.

2. Our first purpose is to form a strategic consensus among our friends in the Middle East. When we are all agreed that the overriding priority in the Middle East is checking the Soviet military thrust toward Persian Gulf oil, the countries of the area will cooperate in the strengthening of the U.S. military position on the ground, and new impetus will be generated to resolve the Arab-Israeli conflict.

*Or:* The unresolved Arab-Israeli and Israeli-Palestinian conflicts

10

are themselves a part of the security threat. The Soviets will exploit them to enhance the Soviet and radical positions in the area. Ordering social and economic change is part of maintaining the independence of the states in the area. The Soviets will exploit disorder as they are trying to do in Iran to improve their strategic position.

3. Nothing would make a greater contribution to the reduction of conflict in the area or to securing the steady flow of oil than a resolution of the Palestinian issue.

*Or:* Conflict is widespread in the Middle East. The United States must support Israel as its strongest strategic asset in the Middle East. Pressing Israel to compromise with those who advocate Palestinian self-determination weakens that asset.

4. The free world depends on the steady flow of Middle East oil.

*Or:* Above all, we will not give in to oil blackmail, as Europe has already done.

Clearly, there are divergent views on what our approach to the Middle East problem should be. There are probably even different views about what the problem is. There is certainly disagreement over whether and, if so, how the various elements of the problem relate to each other.

We cannot resolve all these issues immediately, but I would like to suggest one that we might concentrate on. It is the starting place for a lot of the argument that takes place about the Middle East and Southwest Asia today. In some ways it is the unspoken agenda underlying debate over issues ranging from Awacs to Palestinian self-determination.

The issue is this: Is there one interest we can put above the others because others can be expected to fall into place around it? Or are there interrelationships among those areas of interest that make it necessary to pursue at least several of them more or less simultaneously? If so, what strategy do those interrelationships suggest?

One legitimate approach is to acknowledge that there are indeed five or six significant sets of U.S. interests in the Middle East and Southwest Asia, but to decide that concentrating on one above others is justified and that other issues will fall into place around it. In the mid-1970s, for instance, it was justifiable to explain how pursuit of an Arab-Israeli settlement could be the centerpiece of our strategy in the Middle East. Iran and the Persian Gulf were stable, and there seemed little likelihood of an immediate Soviet threat. In 1974 and 1975, as long as we were actively engaged in pursuing an Arab-Israeli settlement, we developed closer relations with both Israel and the key Arab governments. We succeeded in lifting the oil embargo imposed at the time of the 1973 war by moving toward the Israeli-Syrian disengagement agreement. We dominated the diplomatic stage, and the Soviets were left in second place on that stage. We did not neglect other interests, but they could be tended in the careful conduct of normal bilateral relations. This approach worked because our approach was responsive to priorities of the countries in the area as well as to our own priorities, and because the situation in the area permitted it.

In the early 1980s, after the collapse of the Persian Gulf security system following the Iranian revolution and the Soviet invasion of Afghanistan, it was equally understandable that policy makers would be drawn to concentrate on the security of Persian Gulf oil and the strategic threat to it. There are those today who hold the strong view that the way to approach the Middle East is to impress on our European and Japanese allies and our friends in the Middle East the dangers posed by the Soviet threat. Then, against the background of this strategic consensus, we must press for resolution of other issues such as the Arab-Israeli conflict and oil production levels as essential to the preservation of the strength of the free world and the independence of countries in this area.

A second approach takes the view that the United States cannot deal with the Middle East problem piecemeal in the 1980s when there are so many aspects of our interests in flux at the same time—or, as one analyst put it, where there are so many independent variables. We have to absorb the dramatic change that has taken place since the mid-1970s. Today *all* of our interests are under active challenge in the same period. We could concentrate on one issue in the 1970s because Iran and the Persian Gulf were stable and Afghanistan was still intact as a buffer between the Soviet Union and Southwest Asia. In today's situation, the challenge is to conduct a policy that deals with all of our interests at the same time in conditions of profound social, economic, and political change. We do not have the luxury of addressing one part of the Middle East problem at a time. We cannot deal with each issue separately, even though we want to avoid specific linkages among them. Part of the reason for this is that they are all parts of one world view when seen from the Middle East.

There is nothing inherently right or wrong with one approach or the other. The first approach was appropriate in the mid-1970s, but the second approach is far better suited to the changed situation of the 1980s. The issue for discussion is: What approach gives us the greatest opportunity for pursuing the full range of American interests in the present situation, and how does one decide?

I have one rather simple thought to offer as an initial response to my own question. As we decide on our approach, we need to take into account the interests and perceptions of the Middle Eastern parties. Our power will be greatest and our field for maneuver will be widest if we select an approach that not only enables us to pursue our own interests and to demonstrate our ability to shape events but that also enhances the ability of responsible Middle Easterners to pursue their legitimate goals where we share common purposes.

That may seem so obvious that it is not worth saying. Of course, we often think about other nations' interests when we calculate whether or not it is feasible to achieve our own goals. My point covers more than that. It means a systematic effort to determine exactly where the common ground lies between our interests and theirs. It does not mean an indiscriminate endorsement of their goals. We must define common interests rather than setting our course mainly in terms of our perceptions of the world.

This point is more than academic. There has been over the years within the foreign affairs policy-making community of our government a distinct difference between those who see the world first in terms of U.S.-Soviet relations or, more specifically, nuclear relations, and the regional specialists who emphasize forces at work within a particular region. The global strategist sees the regional specialist missing the big picture; the regional specialist sees the global strategist operating from an unreal picture of the causes of a given conflict. The present administration is no different from others.

I am suggesting an analytical approach for bringing these two schools of thought together. Neither approach by itself is realistic, and the time has come in making policy toward this critical area when we can no longer afford simplistic slogans or bickering between two sets of instincts. We need consensus based on reasoned and consistent analysis.

Consider the following analysis.

A U.S. view of the Soviet threat to this area starts from concern about Soviet control over the flow of oil to the free world. The Soviet invasion of Afghanistan underscores that threat, partly because the turmoil in neighboring Iran tempts Moscow to set up a similar military position in Iran on the Persian Gulf. Because of its global responsibilities, the United States must also be concerned about the effect on the global strategic balance of a successful Soviet move to suppress the independence of a neighboring country by military force

13

and political and administrative takeover. U.S. military planners must consider how they could respond to a direct Soviet military thrust, even though that may be the threat least likely to materialize.

The people of the Middle East, for their part, are keenly aware of Soviet military aggression. The threat to independence and stability in the area looks different, however, to moderate Arabs or to Israelis. In their view the independence, stability, and political orientation of key states in the area are not jeopardized only or even primarily by Soviet military aggression. They may be far more sharply affected by internally generated social, political, and economic forces, as they were in Iran. While keenly aware of the threat of direct Soviet aggression, the people of the area are more immediately concerned about the Soviets exploiting local instability by working through proxies in the area, either through radical parties within the countries or through states allied with the U.S.S.R.

The unresolved Arab-Israeli conflict is also a threat to stability and security in the area. In Arab eyes, it is both an entering wedge for the Soviets to exploit and an issue that radicals can use in attacks on moderate regimes. In the Arab world, the Palestinians themselves might play an influential role in political change. The immediate security threat, as Israelis see it, is from Arab states that they believe reject Israel's existence. Israel sees Moscow backing some of those Arab states to improve its own position.

The flow of oil is more immediately vulnerable both to political pressures related to the unresolved Palestinian issue and to regional violence, whether it be internal revolution, war between states, or sabotage.

In that regional environment, many of the traditional Arab regimes will say that those who would weaken their regimes would be strengthened by too close a strategic relationship with the United States if the United States is not seen to be dealing with issues that are of political and security concern to them. They also believe that the world community will have to deal with direct Soviet aggression diplomatically—successfully or unsuccessfully—as in Afghanistan, since it is unlikely that any power will feel able to confront the Soviet Union militarily on its own back doorstep. In any case, they have no interest in becoming a Vietnam-style battleground.

Given the perceptions of the states in the region, the kind of cooperation we can expect from those states in dealing with issues of concern to us will depend in part on how we deal with security issues of concern to them such as their own internal or national security or the Arab-Israeli conflict. The judgment by Middle Eastern states of external power is most likely to be affected by which world power can concretely turn the course of events in the Middle East. That judgment is at least as likely to be influenced by who can help bring about an honorable and secure Palestinian settlement or by ability to ward off internal enemies as it is by the balance of nuclear power, which is beyond their competence. The Israeli-Palestinian conflict deserves solution in its own right, but how it is resolved and who resolves it will affect the international and domestic orientation of key states, their stability, and their relationships with the superpowers. Although we may disagree over certain specific objectives, we share a common interest in a negotiated settlement that all key states can accept.

Power may also be measured by the ability to provide what these societies need economically and technologically to transform themselves into modern nations. How they will use their economic power will reflect their relations with the superpowers, their views of efforts to deal with issues of concern to them, and even superpower roles in the North-South dialogue. We have a common interest in contributing to constructive growth and orderly change.

Given the diversity of American interests in this area, we must expect that they will, from time to time, confront us with conflicting demands. The challenge to those who make our foreign policy is to find ways to minimize those conflicts, to conduct a policy in this area that will permit us to pursue all of our interests without being forced to make choices among them.

The clearest example of the kind of choice I am talking about stems from the fact that our unchanging support for Israel's security sometimes puts us on a course opposed by even the moderate Arab nations, as was the case when they imposed the embargo on oil shipments following the October 1973 war. Another less obvious example is that we share with most of the moderate nations in this area recognition of a need for an American military capability in the area, but many of the governments there feel that too obvious an American presence on the ground could produce the very instability that outside influences could exploit and that we are trying to prevent.

There are two ways to approach a choice of this kind. One is to choose one interest over another; the other is to look for ways of enlarging the field for finding mutually satisfactory solutions. It is worth considering whether taking the legitimate interests of responsible parties in the Middle East into account will not significantly increase our field of maneuver and enable us to find resolutions that avoid choosing among our interests.

I would suggest as a starting point for discussion the proposition that the United States in the 1980s will need to pursue each of its principal interests actively and simultaneously.

## How to State Our National Purpose

We must now address the question of explaining our national purpose in terms of relatively simple objectives. This is necessary if we are to shape the national consensus that will be essential for the conduct of policy toward this volatile and controversial area.

It is clear that if we choose to put one of these interests out front and let others fall into place around it, that will become the focal point for crystallizing a national consensus. For instance, blocking the Soviets or achieving an Arab-Israeli settlement could become rallying points for public support. If, however, we conclude that we must pursue the full range of our interests at the same time, the question then becomes how a president synthesizes that policy in a simple statement of purpose as he seeks a political mandate for it.

It is, of course, appealing to rally the nation behind the objective of reestablishing confidence in American power. But the complex situation in the Middle East raises the question, What is applicable American power? The American strategic umbrella is fundamental, but the power of American diplomacy may have done more directly to alter the course of history through the five Arab-Israeli agreements signed from 1974 to 1979. On the other hand, American technology and managerial skill may demonstrate more power to transform societies and economies.

It is also appealing to rally consensus around the objective of building a peaceful world. That, however, raises the question in the Middle East and in the rest of the developing world, What is peace? In the Arab-Israeli context we have now reached the point at which we are defining peace not just as the formal end of war and not just as the codification of a state of peace in a treaty. We have now incorporated in the meaning of peace the willingness to establish normal relations between states, and the Egyptian-Israeli peace treaty includes annexes defining a process of normalization of relations between the peoples of the two countries.

In the last quarter of this century, however, we hear voices urging us to an even wider vision of how to deal with a world in which power is increasingly diffused and in which the gravest problems reach well beyond the conventional definitions of peace and questions of the balance of power, important as those questions remain.

For instance, these voices say, peacemaking must begin with a new vision of what peace is. From one quarter after another, we hear the affirmation that peacemaking is not just the act of establishing a preponderance of military power to enforce peace or ending war or preventing violent conflict. We hear that peacemaking must be rooted in removing the causes of conflict and even addressing the basic questions of human security and survival.

The point was put this way in the Brandt Commission report in 1979: "In the global context true security cannot be achieved by a mounting buildup of weapons—defence in the narrow sense—but only by providing basic conditions for peaceful relations between nations, and solving not only the military but also the nonmilitary problems which threaten them." In an unofficial comment, an Egyptian made the point to me earlier this year: "For you to define the threat only as you see it and not to understand how we see it is intellectual imperialism. If you ignore the hopes and fears of our people, you cannot expect to be strong here."

The question is whether some synthesis of national purpose toward the Middle East is possible as we begin to reflect on the relationship between our diplomatic, economic, and military power and our ability to help establish peace in the Middle East in the most forward-looking sense of the word "peace." While it is not the whole picture, it may be worth thinking about how much peacemaking is a form of power and what peacekeeping requires of us.

To be more specific, the United States in the last two decades of this century needs to give at least as much attention to strengthening its peacemaking arsenal as it does to assuring its military power. We need to agree among ourselves that peacemaking, too, is a form of power. To have power is to have the ability to affect the course of events. The experience of the mid-1970s in the Middle East, when the United States mediated the signing of five Arab-Israeli agreements, was that American ability to influence the course of events and its position relative to the Soviet Union were strengthened. Of course, it is essential that we continue to develop our military strength; we have no choice in that. Where we as a nation do have a choice is whether we equally develop a vision of real peace, both at home and abroad, as part of our national objective.

Some problems are not resolved from the deck of an aircraft carrier. If we have to resort to military force to get our way, we may already have lost.

Most Americans understand that we will be strongest in an area like the Middle East in conditions of peace and relative stability. The Soviets thrive on conditions of conflict. Peacemaking may be our first and most effective line of defense.

What might such a consensus mean for policy and for the way we organize ourselves to conduct policy? On the policy front it might mean, for instance, that:

• In Lebanon, we would not stop with the efforts of a presidential emissary to prevent escalation of military conflict. We would give even more effort to helping Lebanon restore national unity in a way that meets the needs of the Lebanon of today and tomorrow.

• We would put a secure and just resolution of the Israeli-Palestinian conflict high on our agenda and seek to broaden the negotiations to win wider Arab support.

• We would intensify our talks with Saudi Arabia and Algeria on issues of the North-South dialogue.

• We might give priority in certain countries to as wide-ranging a discussion as sensitivities would permit to the real threats to internal security, although there are practical difficulties in launching into that subject.

• We might give priority to resolving the Saharan conflict in the West, and we might redouble international pressure against the Soviet presence in Afghanistan.

• We need to give new thought to arms limitation for the more distant future, especially the control of nuclear weapons. In the meantime, we must act with consensus on the legitimate defensive needs of our friends.

### Are We Equipped?

The issues on that agenda may not sound all that new, but they would be new if they were all pursued with energy, with skill, and with coherence as issues of high national priority.

All of this is said with deep concern, because I have to raise the question immediately whether we have the structure or the political base within our political and governmental systems for the conduct of such a policy. Let me underscore that I am not talking about whatever problems the present administration may or may not be having in organizing its foreign policy machinery. I am speaking from twenty years of involvement. I am addressing more fundamental issues.

In the executive branch there are two essential requirements. The critical requirement is the full personal involvement of the president and the secretary of state in setting strategy and in following through. The degree of tactical involvement may vary, but only a command of the complex interrelationships among our interests and the main Middle Eastern interests will produce the sensitive decisions a coherent policy requires. Only that degree of involvement at the top demonstrates that an issue is one of high national priority.

The second requirement in the executive branch is an organizational structure that can coordinate among the departments and agencies involved in the complex strands of bureaucratic perspective and interest that inevitably find lives and connections of their own when so many separate American interests are involved. This coordination is essential both for orderly decision making and for coherent follow-up. It involves coordination at all levels within the National Security Council system, including the president and all the cabinet and subcabinet members with interests and significant programs in the Middle East and Southwest Asia. My experience has been that this bureaucratic machinery is necessary, but that it will work easily or not at all, depending on whether the president and the secretary of state are heavily involved or are obviously pushing the problem off on the bureaucracy.

In the Congress and at our polling booths, consider how often judgments are reached about the Middle East on the basis of a tug-of-war between interest groups rather than on the basis of a serious effort to achieve bipartisan consensus about our interests in the Middle East. Establishing such a consensus is a complicated process. It requires serious attention among the leaders and committees of the Congress. I would suggest tentatively, however, that it depends even more heavily on the evolution of a national consensus. While each member of Congress bears responsibility for leadership in public debate, heavy responsibility falls on a president and his key advisers for explaining to the American people what is at stake, for laying out clearly our choices and their consequences, and for setting a clear national policy. We have heard many foreign policy speeches over the years, but rarely have we heard a searching discussion from the highest levels of our government of what is at stake for the United States in the Middle East and Southwest Asia to lead us in the effort to develop a national consensus.

### Issues for Discussion

As an agenda for discussion, I pose these three issues:

1. Will the Middle East claim high-priority attention and dominate the world stage for Americans in the 1980s? Priority is important. Movement toward peace in the Middle East occurred only after a

war that threatened vital interests and only when the secretary of state and the president became personally involved.

2. How should the United States assign priority or deal with the interrelationships among our major interests in this area? What should be our basic policy approach?

3. How can this approach be synthesized in a statement of national purpose around which our leaders can build a political mandate for their policy?

My purpose is as much to identify and to sharpen issues as it is to test the ingredients of consensus. Too often in the discussion of Middle East issues we end up wrapped around the axle of today's events. Our purpose here is to examine the basic issues that will be here long after today's events have been superseded by the events of another day.

## QUESTIONS AND ANSWERS

DALE TAHTINEN, American Enterprise Institute: Do you think the Israeli strike against the Iraqi nuclear facilities, particularly in combination with the Lebanese problem, might involve the president and the secretary of state to the extent that a higher priority might be put on decisions regarding the Middle East?

MR. SAUNDERS: I would like to hear your views as to whether they should become involved. There is a serious argument that the president should not become so involved in so much detail. Maybe you could address yourself to that point. Does this area require that kind of attention, or is it better left to the secretary of state and people below him?

MR. TAHTINEN: It depends on how strongly the present decision makers feel the Middle East affects our economic program.

MR. SAUNDERS: That is an interesting perspective. Are there economists here who would like to address the question of how events in the Middle East may cut across the top of the president's priority list, namely, the health of our own economy as a base for conducting foreign policy? Is this the way national priorities are assigned when there is a tough trade-off between high-priority domestic issues and international issues?

Robert Lieber, Woodrow Wilson Center: That is a good issue: To what extent will events in the Middle East have an economic impact? We are in a situation in which we oscillate between periods of energy glut and periods of energy crisis. We are experiencing a glut right now, but there is every reason, as you implied, to assume that the system is vulnerable to shocks. Our experience of two serious past shocks has been that they sharply affect the economic health of all the oil-consuming economies. Another shock would once again tighten all the constraints that are related to the problems of stagflation, which we and the Europeans, in particular, have been grappling with over the last eight years. There is every reason to assume that that kind of thing would recur and, as a result, would constrain the domestic economic policies of any government. This possibility guarantees that the Middle East and energy issues are likely to remain well toward the top of the agenda despite temporary oscillations in the nature of the energy problem and in our options to deal with it.

Mr. Saunders: How would the economists involved in putting together the president's current economic program relate the issues that you mentioned to the follow-up success of their program, if the Congress acts over the weeks in ways roughly consistent with the president's recommendations?

Mr. Lieber: There is no way the economists can deal with it satisfactorily. If they base their predictions on what has been happening in one particular period—either a period of glut or a period of crisis—it does not serve well over the longer haul. My guess would be that the administration economists are projecting on the basis of a surprise-free and shock-free future, in which there are no extraneous events to mess up their calculations. The Achilles heel of all of that is exactly such outside shocks, which are more conceivable than not over a period of several years.

Mr. Saunders: Is there anybody who would like to address additional dimensions of this particular subject before we move on?

Jerry Greene, Seven Springs Center: I sense that, as you said, the administration will try to put a *cordon sanitaire* around all difficult foreign policy problems, including the ones we are discussing today, until the political process involving the Congress produces some kind of economic policy that will last for a few years. Congress is sustained in that train of thought by a strong view that Israel is quite capable of dealing with most of the problems that will come up. It also believes that it will be far more useful to the pursuit of American interests not to take on some of the more difficult issues of self-determination and political accommodation to the national interests of other states in the area. The body politic in our own society has a built-in lag that will be hard to overcome.

MR. SAUNDERS: The issue is beginning to be joined here. Dale Tahtinen raised the question at the outset whether individual events will force the top leadership to pay attention to the Middle East. Bob Lieber expanded that a little bit to indicate that the success of the president's economic program will depend on the presence or absence of unexpected shocks. Now Jerry Greene is suggesting that there may be many in Congress who feel that if we are just lucky enough to avoid any of those more immediate events that drive us to the Middle East, probably the national priorities would allow us to let the situation in the Middle East go its own way for some period of time at least, until the administration was ready to address it.

MR. GREENE: The president will have to depend on people who share the view that there really is no problem we need to address in the Middle East in order to get his economic program through. Once he has had the benefit of their support in getting his economic program through, what are they going to do then?

HISHAM SHARABI, Georgetown University: Jerry Greene is pointing to something much deeper than reluctance on the part of Congress. The lag is between the capacity of the administration to address itself to objective American interests abroad, particularly in the Middle East, with the burden of a domestic pressure that sometimes conflicts with those interests. Let me give an example of an Arab perception of that. I take Weber's definition of interests: material as well as ideal, or nonmaterial interests, or principles. The United States, in regard to the Arab-Israeli conflict, has suffered severely in Arab eyes where principles, that is ideal interests, are concerned. I would cite lack of support for the basic principle of self-determination; silence about the expropriation of land by conquest; nonaction with regard to oppression and outright military aggression; the use of American weapons in clear violation of agreements with the United States. All these considerations may be, in part at least, the result of a very critical lag between the perception of American interests and their active pursuit.

LANDRUM BOLLING, Council on Foundations: You raised a question that ties in with what the previous two speakers said when asked whether the president has the political freedom to pursue actively the search for a comprehensive settlement. This is the most critical of all your questions. During the last several administrations, substantial achievements were made, but they came on the heels of war and very great shocks to our national interest. Our presidents were not able to move on these questions prior to those crises. There is something fundamentally wrong in our general internal political situation, at least as perceived by and acted on by the president and the Congress, that makes it difficult if not impossible for them to pursue consistently, over a long period of time, our national interest and the resolution of these problems. How can we go about developing a greater national political consensus that would free the president and his colleagues to pursue a consistent policy? This towers over all of the other questions that you have put before us.

MR. SAUNDERS: Let me ask you to analyze for a moment two parts of the question. The first part, thrown out by Jerry Greene, is to analyze the roots of the argument that we should not assign high priority to this area. The second is the question that Landrum Bolling just posed, that is, How do we go about developing a consensus, whatever that consensus may be?

NICK THIMMESCH, journalist, American Enterprise Institute: If the administration perceives our national interest in the Middle East as oil and the protection of it, has it not shown that its approach is to use military force to protect that oil? It has not shown much interest in getting into the Palestinian issue or into the resolution of the Arab-Israeli conflict or even into settling the Lebanese crisis.

MR. SAUNDERS: What are the roots of that line of argument?

MR. THIMMESCH: That is what the administration has shown so far.

MR. SAUNDERS: I am not thinking about this administration, whether it has or it has not, but that is a line of argument current among some in this administration. What are the intellectual roots of that argument? It is not a new argument.

MR. THIMMESCH: It is protecting economic interest—oil—and not seeing the social or political factors in the Middle East, only seeing the situation in military terms.

ALFRED MOSES, private attorney in Washington: The roots may be more practical and historical than conceptual. The crisis over oil arose at the same time as the Israeli-Arab war of 1973. The focus of Henry Kissinger and the State Department thus was the resolution of the Israeli-Arab conflict as a critical ingredient in assuring the continuing flow of oil. Since then we have seen, as a result of the invasion of Afghanistan, of the fall of the shah, of the Iranian-Iraqi war, that there are other factors that can potentially or actually affect the flow of oil. Policy has, however, been shaped by our concern for a continuing flow of oil to the Western world, not necessarily to the United States per se, but to the whole industrialized West, of which we are a part. I do not know that intellectual antecedents to that policy exist other than in the practical historical framework that I referred to.

PETER CHASE, Mobil Oil: I was under the impression that the use of military force to acquire Middle East oil went back at least before World War I, when the British and the Germans were in competition for Iranian oil. It was certainly a major factor in both the whole Middle East campaign in World War II and the tripartite attack on the Egyptians in 1956.

MR. SAUNDERS: We have talked about our concern for the Soviet threat in Afghanistan and for the flow of oil. Are some of you suggesting that perhaps those are our two principal concerns and that they indeed ought to become the rallying points for American policy in this area? Or is our concern somewhat broader?

BARRY RUBIN, Georgetown University Center for Strategic and International Studies: First, a brief remark on the intellectual roots of this new view. The concept that the 1950s was a time of great success for American policy because, after all, things did not go wrong then, is counterposed to the view that the policies of the 1950s alienated the third world and opened up many of the problems of the ensuing years. A second root is the concept of the indirect approach to projecting American power, which is often referred to ironically as the Nixon doctrine. It is said that this did not work, because of what happened in Iran. Therefore, as the argument runs, if we want to do something right, we have to do it ourselves. A third perception is that American unwillingness to use power, as in Iran and Nicaragua, was a mistake, that in fact people respect those who use power and join their side. Therefore, power must be used and used directly by the United States. One often hears the argument that the Saudis and other Gulf Arabs say in public that they are against

24

American bases, but in private they tell us differently. I am still waiting after a number of years for somebody to tell me some of these things in private, but this is what some of my colleagues insist.

There is a very clear, very well-organized concept, which is essentially dominant now, that the problem is not so much what we do but how we do it. Everyone here will agree that the Soviets are not nice people and that the expansion of their influence is not in our interest. Then the question comes, What means do we use to cope with that? Obviously, the means that are being proposed are very direct kinds of military responses. We attribute almost every kind of instability to Soviet intervention. When some of us say we propose different means, we propose indirect means, we propose supporting oil-producing countries and taking into account their concerns, we are not saying we do not have the same ends in mind. We are not saying we are not concerned about oil, we are not concerned about the Soviets; we are simply saying that the direct procedures that are suggested do not work, are short-sighted, and are the cause of greater problems. Maybe the method rather than the ends is the key issue here. One can say, for example, that American policy in the 1950s was a great success, but let's go back and look at what actually happened. When the United States was at the height of its power, it certainly could not prevent the Iraqi revolution of 1958. We could list ten other major upheavals in the Middle East. People believe that certain methods work simply because their failures happened long enough ago that no one remembers them anymore.

MR. SAUNDERS: When we select the means, though, we have a certain strategy in mind. Do you have in mind the strategy of simply thwarting Soviet aggression, or do you have in mind some broader set of objectives? The means we choose will depend on our perception of our interests and what our priorities are among those interests.

MR. RUBIN: One clear and simple question is, What is the greatest threat to stability in the Persian Gulf? Now the argument is that the Soviets pose the greatest threat to stability in the Persian Gulf, both directly, in subversion, and indirectly, through terrorism. I would argue, and I think other people would argue, that the greatest threat is internal upheavals resulting from discontinuities of social and economic modernization. That leads in very different directions. What is causing the instability and what to do about it become quite different questions.

MR. SAUNDERS: If that is your concern, how then do you regard the other U.S. interests that I have laid out? Are they related to that particular set of concerns, or can you handle that particular set of concerns by itself?

MR. RUBIN: Obviously, they are interrelated. One problem is that the means may become counterproductive. If we were to say that internal instability, not necessarily Soviet-fostered, is the greatest threat in various states, and we applied great pressure for bases, for example, or for direct American intervention, then that can in fact increase internal instability and can be counterproductive. What I am worried about is that the interpretation may lead us in the opposite direction from the one we want to go in.

DAVID NEWSOM, Georgetown University: Granted that the Middle East has an importance that may well transcend other interests, nevertheless, the United States at some point has to make a decision about the broad allocation of its resources and its capacity. In this discussion we are assuming an infinite capacity of the United States to respond in the Middle East, an infinite capacity of support from our allies, from the peoples in the area. We have to make much tougher decisions than that implies.

Let's go back to the question of national consensus. One question that needs to be approached is whether from the political standpoint of any administration there is an opportune time to seek a national consensus on the Middle East, a time that is not obstructed by elections.

MR. SAUNDERS: Tell us where the Middle East fits in with our global perspectives. You are as well equipped as anybody in this room to do that; you have been through it.

MR. NEWSOM: As long as we are still dependent on foreign sources of energy, although it is an energy dependence that we hope can diminish over the next three or four decades, the Middle East will still be very important. With regard to allocation of resources, it should not necessarily get a higher priority than the defense of the industrial base in Europe. We also are approaching a situation in which the Pacific base is almost of greater interest to us than Europe because of our trade and other interests. The Middle East is, in a sense, temporarily important because of one resource it has. We must as a nation face up to the fact that maybe we cannot do all of the things that we want to do in all of these areas. We will have to make some very tough decisions, and we will have to move away from our long-held assumption that we, as a nation, can do what we want to do wherever we want to do it.

MR. SAUNDERS: It is true that the Middle East has always been important to us mainly because it has been important to Europe and Japan because of the oil. What about another dimension, though, the political orientation? What difference does it make to the strategic balance how close key nations in the area are to the Soviet Union or to us, apart from the question of whether or not oil is cut off? Is that something we should give high priority in our calculations?

MR. NEWSOM: Over the last three years we have been on quite a different wavelength from that of the Europeans in looking at the problems of the Middle East. We are on a different wavelength both in looking at politics and in seeking assured access to the resources of the Middle East. By American logic, the Europeans should be even more concerned and should be even more prepared to contribute to a military posture that would deter the Soviets in the Middle East. That is just not the case, however. I worry about a strategy that centers on major American deployment to the Middle East because we have to go through Europe to get to the Middle East, and we cannot be sure of the support of the Europeans.

MR. SAUNDERS: You are talking there about a military deployment rather than a diplomatic deployment, if I may coin a new phrase.

MR. NEWSOM: The Europeans would welcome, as they have generally, a forceful American diplomacy in the area. They have views of what that should embrace that we are not yet prepared to adopt, but they would welcome it.

HOWARD COTTAM, American University: It seems to me that if we are talking about consensus on any one avenue, whether it is on the military, or on oil, or on whatever, we are losing something very important. You are talking about the long term, not just the direction this administration seems to be turning. Let me turn from those basic principles you have been talking about. We have begun to knock down all of the efforts to globalize that we have been building up for a long time, because they do not seem to have solved some of these nasty problems. We begin to eschew not only intervention by the United Nations to solve problems, but intervention by the World Bank and the International Monetary Fund as well. The World Bank wants to assist in finding oil elsewhere, for example. The International Monetary Fund has been trying some new approaches, which apparently we abhor. It seems to me that if we are going to get a consensus we have to draw back on some of those basic principles you mentioned as well.

MR. GREENE: If I understood Landrum Bolling correctly he asked what we can do to change the grid-lock that sometimes seems to be on this. One thing that could accomplish that is to extend to congressional elections the public financing procedures that are provided for presidential elections. Any effort to extend public financing to congressional elections seems to me to have been blocked by just the people who have an interest in keeping the grid-lock on some of the things that we are talking about. The capacity of special interests on a wide front to affect the attitudes of members of the Congress through the funding of their election campaigns would be considerably diluted, if not eliminated, by having all congressional campaigns financed by the public treasury except as the congressmen can put their own money into it.

ROBERT GOLDWIN, American Enterprise Institute: I admire your attempt to discuss this passionate issue dispassionately and to pose abstract questions that would give a form to the discussion and that might get past certain distortions of emotion. I see, however, that the attempt really does not work. There are people here with deeply held emotional positions who use your abstract formal scheme to advance arguments of a quite different sort. For instance, our colleague from Georgetown spoke about the Arab view, which really calls into question the principles of the United States and the honesty of the United States in pursuit of its principles. He listed four principles having to do with self-determination, acquisition of territory by force, human rights, and the use of U.S. weapons contrary to law. On these very points there is and has been a strong moral consensus in the United States on the side of Israel. There has been a clear belief on the part of the American people as a whole—not some distortion created by the contributions of Jewish money to congressional candidates, as was implied here—that Israel is on the side of self-determination, that the Arab enemies of Israel wanted to drive Israel into the sea and prevent it from determining its own fate in establishing its own political entity. As for human rights, the reason there is strong U.S. popular consensus on the side of Israel is that it is thought of as a nation that really respects human rights. There is no evidence that Israel's enemies have any concern for human rights; they do not see human rights in their countries, and they speak of human rights only with regard to the situation on the West Bank. As for acquiring territory by force, everybody remembers that the Arabs would have driven the Israelis into the sea if they had had enough force. Whether the use of U.S. weapons is according to law or not depends on whether they are being used in defense of Israel. Most Americans consider it obvious that they are being used in the defense of Israel. They also wonder about the Soviet supply of weapons on the other side.

It is important that we keep in mind, as you strive, admirably, as I said, to present a formal structure for considering this subject, that most people will immediately distort it into a forum for a different kind of discussion of the situation.

MR. SAUNDERS: It is still worth striving for a discussion of what some of the principles really mean. Anybody who tries to apply them in the real world learns very quickly that they are not easy to apply. In the real world, circumstances shape the way they are applied, but a discussion of how the principle applies to a given situation is precisely what I hope for. I would like to hear from Ambassador Tahseen Basheer before we close.

TAHSEEN BASHEER, American Enterprise Institute and Egyptian Ambassador-designate to Canada: I have some difficulty with your proposition on two grounds. You keep talking about the Soviets, but you have not asked yourself who invited the Soviets to the area. The Soviets were not in the area: they were invited to the area. When they were invited to the area, it was an American failure to deal with the problems of the area that invited the Soviets in. That is the starting point. When the Soviets were kicked out of some parts of the area, it was the people of those parts of the area who kicked them out. What was missing in your analysis and in parts of certain episodes of American policy was the people of the third world, the Arabs in this case; the people do not count. You talk about us as the Suez Canal, as oil, as the Persian Gulf, as the Arabs of the Persian Gulf—the people do not count.

The second point is that you dealt with your system without even a reference to your allies, whether you want to live with an American international system, in a global system, even with the Western allies. To what extent do you argue, do you have a dialogue with your allies in the area and with your allies in Europe? Whatever the Europeans do, you always say they have succumbed to Arab blackmail. Now they answer back, What kind of blackmail have you succumbed to? The question that America has to raise is, Are we going to pursue whatever policy is conceived from time to time, from administration to administration, or are we going to deal with this within a global system that puts certain guidelines, certain regulations on all of us, small and big, to gear the world effort constructively? Lacking this, we will be shifting at random. Again, internally, the question of the people, particularly after the Iranian revolution, is very important. A policy cannot be built on some shah or some shiek or some prime minister. The interests of the people must be considered. That has not been coming. When America invested in a healing process, whether under Roosevelt for self-determination or under Carter for a peace process between Arabs and Israelis, the Soviet Union lost a lot, because it did not use this healing power and these creative policies. Is the United States pursuing a defensive strategy for the future or a constructive, creative structure that takes the interests of the people, the interests of its allies, as a part of that policy?

MR. SAUNDERS: This is a useful point from which to take off into our future conversations. One of the central suggestions I made here today that will follow through in our later discussions is, What does it contribute to analyze the interests of the people of the Middle East to find the areas of common purpose and to build American policy partly from that analysis of common purpose and partly from an understanding of our own interests?

MICHAEL P. HAMILTON, canon, Washington Cathedral: As a resident of and long-time follower of an equally passionate dispute in Northern Ireland, I learned two things—that the consensus can be wrong and that any consensus deserves evaluation and reevaluation in terms of neutrals. I cannot be persuaded that just because a consensus has been arrived at, that this is necessarily what should be. There is no substitute for what Harold Saunders is proposing, an attempt at a principled, dispassionate exchange of opinions. It is very dangerous to question the motives of those who attempt to abuse such an exchange. Even though we do not totally achieve success, the venture itself is always worth supporting. It is also the only way the American people themselves can get above the propaganda on both sides to understand something of the history and the factual realities of this situation.

MR. SAUNDERS: We have obviously only begun to scratch the surface of the issues that we will continue to address in our discussions.

# 2

# Forces of Change in the Middle East: Constraints and Opportunities for U.S. Foreign Policy

A CONVERSATION WITH HAROLD H. SAUNDERS

*June 22, 1981*

The rapid pace of change brings with it the threat of instability that can profoundly alter the character of a nation and its orientation among the superpowers. It can jeopardize independence by inviting the involvement of the superpowers. I have chosen this focus for our conversation today because we as a people seem to have difficulty relating to change in other parts of the world, sometimes with good reason but sometimes because we do not stop to analyze what is going on and what the causes of change are. It is indeed difficult to say that we have an interest in stability and then to say that we need a policy for dealing with change that almost by its nature causes instability.

The issue before the United States, then, is how to conduct a policy for pursuing its interests in the context of widespread and rapidly accelerating change. Our objectives today, therefore, are: to note briefly the nature and principal directions of change; to discuss how our interests are really affected; and to lay out for further conversation some of the issues and policy choices posed as we decide what our posture should be toward change in the area.

## The Nature and Direction of Change

The Middle East and Southwest Asia is experiencing the problems and dislocations common to the developing world, but at a pace that makes it even more difficult than usual to keep social, economic, and political elements of change in some kind of balance. It is not change itself that necessarily endangers American interests but the upheaval that can result within a country when the evolution of political institutions and leadership do not keep pace with change in other areas.

Although the countries of this area vary widely, oil producers and non-oil producers alike face in some combination the normal problems of rapid population growth (2 to 3 percent a year) and limited food-producing land, lack of water, rising urban unemployment, rural poverty, and expectaions of higher living standards.

At the same time, there is much that is unique in this region because of the sharp increase in substantial oil revenues, particularly in those countries with large oil exports and with relatively small populations. Although this poses different developmental problems for each country, the rise in oil revenues has made it possible for countries with oil and countries without oil alike to embark on ambitious development plans.

Even countries that do not export substantial quantities of oil achieved impressive annual rates of increase (6 to 8 percent) in gross domestic product through the 1970s. Much of the financing came indirectly from oil revenues.

As development expenditures increase, governments will be making decisions about development strategies that will affect the social and political balances within their countries for the remainder of the century and beyond. In the countries with high oil revenues it may be that the abundance of resources, as in our own experience, will cushion the social and political consequences of some waste and mismanagement. But even they will not be immune to judgment, as became apparent in Iran.

The consequences of these decisions about development strategy cut across the entire spectrum of a society's life and character and affect the stability it maintains through the process of growth. A primary area for potential instability stems from the possible widening of *inequalities within the society*, with potentially profound political consequences. There may well be a widening of the gap between rural and urban dwellers, the gap between the urban poor and those participating in the modern economy, and the gap between those who do and do not participate in political decision making.

Rapid economic development has been accompanied by *structural changes* in the sinews holding societies together. Examples are the erosion of the traditional merchant middle class as a social force, the emergence of a new middle class in the evolution of the civilian and military bureaucracies, and, in some of the more traditional societies, the erosion of tribal relationships and the codes by which leadership was established.

Rapid economic and social change has also had its impact on *political institutions*. Political instability is a fact of life in many countries of the region, but its causes vary from country to country. One common denominator is the issue of participation by broad segments of the population in guiding the direction of change. The strength of separate nationalist identities within existing nation-states poses a particular challenge to central authority in these states.

Out of the development process come needs and decisions that will affect *relationships among the nations of the area* that can have profound social and political consequences. There is a dramatically increasing interdependence evident in the flow of oil revenues into the development programs of non-oil countries, in the reverse movement of labor in the area, and in the remittances that flow back home from those workers. On the political-military front, the Egyptian-Israeli peace treaty opens the door to a further interdependence of two new sorts; the shift of resources from military to development purposes and the kind of change that would come from normalization of relations.

One major reaction to change has been the *reassertion of cultural and religious identity, particularly Islamic*. The Iranian revolution was a notable example, but we see elements of an Islamic resurgence in practically every Islamic nation today.

### How Our Interests Are Affected

The question we have to ask ourselves in light of the situation I have just described is exactly how our interests are affected by these changes. We do not have to—indeed we should not—feel responsible for the process of change in other countries. One of the broader meanings of the principle of self-determination is that peoples have not only the right to determine in some way their form of government but also the full responsibility for determining how they will direct the course of development for their generation and the generations that follow.

To begin, it is necessary for us to define with greater precision exactly what our interests are. I identified three dimensions of our interests—independence, stability, and political orientation. Let's look at these more carefully.

*Independence* is a way of saying freedom from Soviet or other outside domination. It is worth noting three specific concerns. First,

33

the breach of any nation's independence, as in Afghanistan, has profound consequences for the future of order in the world. It is one of the hard, cold interests of the United States to uphold the principles of the UN Charter. Those words were written on the threshold of the nuclear era with the tragedy of two world wars fresh in mind. They were meant to govern relations between nations for sound reason.

Second, expansion of Soviet control in any form affects the global strategic balance. Even though there are no strategic commodities like oil in Afghanistan, it makes a difference that the world sees the Soviet Union as the advancing and the United States as the retreating power. In addition, the presence of Soviet military forces in Afghanistan increases the direct threat to Pakistan, to Baluchistan, to parts of Iran, and ultimately to the Persian Gulf.

Third, specifically in Southwest Asia, Soviet control in the oil-producing countries or at the Straits of Hormuz would give the Soviet Union control over the flow of oil that is literally vital to our allies.

Before we leave this concern for the independence of these countries, we must examine briefly exactly how their independence might be curbed and exactly how our interests would be affected. In other words, exactly what is the threat to our interest?

The Soviet administrative and military invasion of Afghanistan is easy to identify as loss of Afghan independence. The invasion came a year and a half after a takeover by an indigenous communist-style party that was imbued with the Marxist-Leninist ideology and approach. The coup, however, seemed to grow out of Afghan social and political dynamics and did not seem to be engineered from Moscow. The Afghans are denied the freedom to set their own policies and to determine their own relationships. The United States is denied freedom to work out with Afghan authorities acting freely in their own interests a relationship built on whatever interests we have in common.

In South Yemen, the degree of Soviet influence is substantial, but the degree of Soviet control is less clear. The Soviet military have formal access to naval facilities. Soviet, Cuban, and East European advisers play a significant role in South Yemeni military capability. In addition to the Soviet presence, there is an indigenous Marxist government, as there was in Afghanistan after the April 1978 coup. Soviet control is by no means certain, but the combination of the government's own posture and the Soviet presence has so far prevented a normal relationship.

Iraq and Syria, also signatories of Soviet friendship treaties, have

Soviet-equipped military forces. The governments are controlled by the Ba'ath party, a non-Marxist Arab party with a socialist bent. While they may listen to the Soviets because on occasion they want Soviet support or arms, Moscow cannot be said to exercise any degree of control.

In Iran, two issues arise. First, there is the long-term possibility that a leftist group might control the government there and involve the Communist party, which has markedly improved its organization and position since the revolution. Depending on the political composition of such a government, Soviet influence would be greater or less. Second, the weakening of central authority opens the door to declarations of autonomy by local authorities and to invitations of Soviet support, which could lead to establishment of puppet regimes.

Finally, there are the liberation movements like the Palestine Liberation Organization (PLO), which the Soviets support materially because of their attack on the established order and their widespread popular support. Those movements wish to retain their independence as any nationalist movement but also will pay some price for support.

The net of this is that our interests are seriously affected mainly when Soviet influence reaches the point at which indigenous leadership no longer independently makes final decisions—where to sell oil, how to relate to neighbors and other powers, how to use their military forces. As long as indigenous leadership retains the capacity to assess its own interests and to make its own decisions, the problems we have to deal with in our relationship with them are not all made in Moscow; they are a combination of local forces and Soviet influence.

The Soviets have most commonly come close to that degree of influence by working politically through internal social and political dynamics. The direct total takeover on the Afghan model is a threat that cannot be ignored, but concentrating on that as the most likely danger will risk overlooking the broader techniques by which the Soviets have gained influence. It would seem to be worth a good deal more effort than we have expended to understand what makes countries vulnerable or resistant to this kind of Soviet-supported influence.

Our second area of concern—*stability and political orientation*—poses a definitional problem right at the outset. How can we speak of stability in the midst of change that is almost inevitably destabilizing to some degree? Yet we use the word repeatedly, so we need to reach some understanding about what our interest is not and what it is. I am also coupling the question of political orientation with that of stability because, in the end, that has a lot to do with determining how we judge the results of political change.

On the one hand, there are some Americans who seem to operate from assumptions suggesting that the U.S. interest lies in protecting the status quo. For instance, some argue that we should somehow have used force or supported the use of force to bring the Iranian revolution under control. The same people argued against any form of U.S. intervention in the earlier 1970s to try to address potential causes of revolution. Others argue that the correct U.S. posture is to back established friendly regimes and to keep opposition elements at arm's length. This is often expressed as "supporting our friends" or "not letting our friends down." Still others see various nationalist or liberation groups mainly as subversive arms of the Soviet Union that must be blocked.

The questions raised by this approach are whether such movements can be stopped, whether trying to block them is worth the cost, and what, if any, would be the exact U.S. role if a blocking effort were made.

On the other hand, there are those who argue that our future in this region will be jeopardized if we use our power to resist change. Secretary of State Cyrus Vance, for instance, addressed this issue in Chicago on May 1, 1979, after a year of revolution in Iran and mounting resistance in Afghanistan to the communist-style government there. He spoke on meeting the challenge of a changing world: Our future, he said, will be endangered if we react in frustration and use our power to resist change in the world or if we employ military power when it would do more harm than good. If we Americans appreciate the extraordinary strengths we have, he went on, and if we understand the nature of the changes taking place in the world, then we have every reason to be confident about our future. Our challenge is to use effectively the various kinds of power and influence we possess to ensure the evolution of these events in the manner least disruptive and most congenial to our interests.

The questions raised by this approach are how the United States can help ensure the evolution of events in nondisruptive ways and what our role should be if events reach the point of imminent threat to our interests.

In other words, there are some who would find stability in coming as close as possible to protecting the status quo by supporting existing regimes. There are others who would find stability in trying to shape change in an orderly way, even if this means some change in the character of regimes. In each case, there is a commitment to the independence and integrity of nations; the difference lies in the approach to the political management of internal change.

Two basic questions, therefore, are: Where does stability lie, and what is the proper focus of the American commitment to support stability?

When we try to determine what we mean by internal stability, we come to the following observations. First of all, we ought to acknowledge honestly that the degree of our concern for stability is partly determined by a government's political orientation. If instability moves a government toward the West, our interest is different from that in the more common situation in which violent change moves a regime toward closer affinity with the U.S.S.R. Our attitude toward the present resistance movement in Afghanistan and our concern about the course of the revolution in Iran make this case.

Next, we should put out in the open our premise that the United States has more going for it than the Soviet Union in a straightforward competition for influence in this region. We simply have more of what the people in the area want. We have a greater potential to cooperate in their development, including an ideology rooted in the elements of self-determination and protection of their full independence. This contrasts to the Soviet objective of imperial domination. Another way of putting the point is in the familiar statement that Americans are builders and thrive on stability, while the Soviets do better exploiting instability to destroy the established order. From this premise flow two key points about our interest in the internal stability of nations in this area.

Negotiated political change is more likely to produce change that is less threatening to our interests than change suppressed by violence or change brought about by violence. One reason for this is that negotiated change is more likely to produce a situation in which common interests are assessed rationally—a situation in which the United States has maximum opportunity to exercise its comparative advantage.

If negotiated political change is a key element in the kind of stability that serves our interests, it follows that the United States has a strong interest in the peaceful, negotiated resolution of internal conflict. We have an interest; we may not be able and we do not have a right to play a role in resolving internal conflict in all cases. Our policy should lead us immediately to questions about how internal conflict can be resolved as early as possible and what role the United States can play. Once again we have returned to the point that peacemaking—in this case, internal peacemaking—can shape events in a way that may protect common interests.

37

## Key Policy Issues

This brings us to the critical question of how far the United States can properly go in addressing the causes of potential internal conflict in other nations. We certainly should not get ourselves in a position of looking as if we think we know more about how to run another country than its own leaders do. In practical political and diplomatic terms, it is also very difficult for our leaders to tell other leaders that they should or should not be managing their elections in one way or another, or that they need to crack down on corruption, or that they should draw opposition elements into the government. There are, however, critical times when our advice and help are asked, as in Iran in 1978 and in Lebanon today.

Whatever the degree of actual U.S. involvement may be, I recommend that the U.S. government make the immediate and potential causes of internal conflict and instability the focus of analytical reporting from the field on a basis of higher priority than is the case at present. Political and economic analysis of the social, political, and economic dynamics of the countries we deal with has been given considerable attention in the past four years. That effort needs to be reaffirmed as a matter of high priority, and it now needs to focus on the immediate and potential causes of internal instability and conflict.

I would further recommend that this subject become part of the occasional conversations among high-level political leaders to show that the United States gives high priority to identifying causes of potential conflict and finding a negotiated resolution before they get beyond control.

Any such exchange could be brought within bounds of propriety by basing it on certain shared interests in the process of change such as these:

- We do want to see people move from lives of poverty to lives in which the genuinely good things of modern life are available.
- Since we have an interest in a negotiated evolution of political institutions, we have an interest in broader participation in decision making that provides constructive avenues for working out dissent.
- We have an interest in development strategies and projects that minimize their becoming objects of political opposition, either because of corruption or because of waste that provokes charges of mismanaging resources.

- We have an interest in the evolution of effective military forces in like-minded countries. This includes the wise use of defense resources in purchasing equipment as well as in effective use of it once purchased.
- We have an interest in the development of new elements of national cohesion as old ones break down.
- We have an interest in American participation in the rapidly growing market for goods and services. Among other reasons, this is critical to paying for imported oil.

### Issues for Discussion

In short, the Middle East and Southwest Asia is one of the fastest changing areas of the developing world today. We need to give far more attention in formulating policy to the dynamics of that change as it may affect American interests and as we may influence it, if at all.

With that larger objective in mind, I suggest that our conversation focus on these three clusters of questions:

- How do we define the degree of Soviet involvement in a country that our interests can tolerate?
- Can social and political revolutions be stopped? Is trying to block them worth the cost? What, if any, would be the exact U.S. role if a blocking effort were made?
- How can the United States ensure the evolution of events in nondisruptive ways? What should the U.S. role be if events reach the point of imminent threat to our interests?

Without a sharper definition of our purpose than has been developed to date, the United States risks involvement in the social, political, and economic dynamics of the Middle East that could work against the very interests we seek to protect.

Let me open the floor to comments of any kind relating to these questions or relating to the analysis of a very complex situation in the area where the manifestations of change are legion.


## QUESTIONS AND ANSWERS

GEORGE ASSOUSA, Carnegie Endowment for International Peace: The United States could not be thinking about intervening positively in the process of change without bringing the private sector in an active way into the foreign policy-making machinery. I would like to keep that part of it in the consideration of the questions that we will be addressing today, because it is central to the question of constructive intervention in the process of change.

MR. SAUNDERS: Our policy has been based for the last seven or eight years, if not longer, on the premise that the American private sector will carry a substantial burden of the American presence in the Middle East. This is self-evident with the increase of investment wealth in this area. These countries will be in the market for the kinds of goods, services, and equipment that the American firms can provide. That is a good thing from the point of view of the national interest. Whether we are talking about the involvement of the American private sector, about the involvement of American government institutions, or about the involvement of the international developmental institutions, the U.S. government needs to assume some responsibility for at least thinking about what makes sense as an overall framework for development within these countries. It must also consider the possible hitches that might cause instability. I am talking about an analytical base from which the U.S. government might play its role, whatever that role might be.

MILTON VIORST, journalist: When a country is having an election, what kind of deliberation goes on in the Department of State and in the White House when the outcome of the election is clearly extremely important to the interests of the United States? After you address that, perhaps you could give us your opinion about what degree of involvement in this kind of internal matter is appropriate for the United States.

MR. SAUNDERS: Elections in other countries represent two different categories of problems. One has to do with the evolution of institutions in that country that permit the involvement of all groups in the society that should play a role in expressing their feelings about the direction society should take. In a well-developed democracy this is not an issue. In other countries, however, it is very much a question of seeing the evolution of institutions that can provide the same kind of political expression that one gets in a democracy, although perhaps through forms quite different from those of Western parliamentary democracy. That is one set of problems one needs to address on the question of how the United States should react to or relate to the electoral process in other countries. There may be structural

40

changes that in one way or another are appropriate subjects of discussion for high political leaders.

The second category of problems is the one you are referring to, and that is, how does the United States position itself to play an appropriate role in the decision-making process of another country? I say an appropriate role, because in many situations, it is not a question of whether the United States will have some influence or not. In some situations, it seems to me that the conduct of American policy during a period of internal debate in another country will in one way or another affect the thinking of some people about how that government has related to the U.S. government. We have to rule out the possibility of our playing no role at all, even if the United States has no intention whatsoever of influencing the course of events inside that other electoral process. Therefore, our government must be very careful at particularly sensitive times about how its actions will be played in another country. It is very difficult, perhaps impossible, to figure out how a particular act by the U.S. government will play in another country. Administrations in this country have enough trouble figuring out how their actions related to domestic American issues will play in one part of the electorate or another. It is a cause of real debate.

My recommendation would be that the United States should, in a period like this, simply settle down to say what it thinks its policy ought to be, to conduct its policies in a nonpolemical, nonantagonistic way. It should go about its business and let the chips fall where they may in the course of the other country's electoral campaign. I see no other way to conduct policy with integrity and with intelligence. I do not think we are smart enough to figure out that one action or another will have one effect or another in somebody else's electoral campaign. I do not limit that to the present situation. I have seen this question come up again and again over twenty years, and I have concluded that this is the only proper thing to do. Do what we should do as the United States, the greatest power in the world, and let the other country figure out how our action relates to its interests.

MR. NEWSOM: I would like to challenge three premises that seem to be implied in what you said. You spoke about negotiated change. I find it difficult to identify any historic development in the Middle East in the last few years that could really be called negotiated change. I wonder if that is a realistic possibility.

MR. SAUNDERS: Let me give an example of a situation that you and

I shared intimately to suggest what I have in mind—namely, Iran. Looking back over the course of the Iranian revolution, we remember that it became an issue late in 1978 whether there was some way to form a regency council and to develop a more broadly participatory group of governmental overseers to work out some kind of change that would not bring the house down, so to speak. Admittedly, it came very late in the game and therefore was almost swept away by the course of events. Let's suppose that someone could have said early in 1978 that the course of events looked as if it could indeed bring the house down if somebody did not get on top of it quickly. That raises the question of how much one can advise a leader of that kind. If the shah had decided that things needed immediate attention and had begun then trying to work out the participation of other elements in the society (we call this liberalizing the government or broadening its base), then perhaps there might have been a chance to get ahead of the game.

This has many ramifications. I do not mean that we should do this. When I say negotiated change, I do not mean necessarily sitting down across the table in a bargaining session, but I mean negotiated change in the sense of change worked out in a political process rather than change brought about in the streets.

MR. NEWSOM: Certainly you and I have seen several efforts at negotiated change. Perhaps I should have said that it is hard to point to one that was successful. I recall efforts in Yemen amd efforts in Lebanon, which brings me to my second point. That is, whether there is not implied in what you are saying an assumption of a greater receptivity on the part of governments in the Middle East to what the United States thinks about their internal organization. That would mean less influence on the part of this country in their internal organizations than we may hope for or than we may even believe is possible.

MR. SAUNDERS: I want to be very clear to avoid the appearance of some sort of sophomoric exercise of trying to work out political structures in other countries. We all know that it is indeed sophomoric even to think in those terms. I am thinking of something on a different plane. Other governments will not take our advice, particularly about what they should or should not do. In some cases, as in Lebanon, they come and plead for it, so it depends on what the situation is. What I am really talking about is elevating the consciousness of governments, including our own, about this process of social, political, and economic change in which they are all enmeshed. The consequences of development strategy should be taken into account. It is a problem of putting the idea into the air so that it becomes something that people think about and do something about. I suggested at the end of my talk that I do not see why the subject put on that basis should be taboo on the agenda for discussions among high-level political leaders. It is taboo for an American president to tell a foreign government what to do. Getting top leaders to think in a certain mode can be a tremendous step forward simply because when a president or a king starts talking about certain problems, that consciousness trickles down. I am not suggesting a panacea; I am simply suggesting a posture for the United States.

AMBASSADOR BASHEER: You raised a very crucial question. Aside from the normal dialogue between countries, the United States must establish a clear policy. There is a common misconception that the United States is the most knowledgeable nation on the Middle East. The record does not support that. I can make an argument that a lot of the instability in the Middle East has resulted from wrong American decisions and from a lack of continuity in U.S. foreign policy.

Who in America knows and can reach decisions of responsibility about the development in Yemen, or in Afghanistan, or in Sudan, or in Egypt, or in Timbuktu? A friend of mine and a former professor, David Lerner, gave us a nice bible on developing societies in the Middle East. He visited me in Cairo four years ago and told me that all his theories were wrong. How would you and the State Department decide that to encourage this class or that class will produce the right political decisions? Unless initiatives were created from the people in the area, how would the United States have brought peace? The United States can encourage certain trends, it can make its stand known. We have a problem on the receiving end understanding American policy in its zig-zags and changes. Americans have a certain lack of humility about their ability to devise a development revolution. No one can be that much on top of development.

The United States can make its policy clear to the countries of the world and then have a dialogue about it, a dialogue of interest. What happens if the United States suggests to my government or to the shah of Iran a certain policy? The United States did that from 1953, when it put him in power; it encouraged a certain policy, and look at the results of it in 1979. Who pays for that? That is the big question. Why pick only 1979? Why not start from the countercoup in 1953? One could argue that for twenty years the United States got goods and oil out of Iran at cheaper prices that made the risk in 1979 worthwhile.

MR. SAUNDERS: I would like to rule out very precisely, as I did in my earlier remarks, any notion that the United States should tell another country how to manage its internal affairs. We do not have the wisdom to do that, and we should not have a policy based on that. People in the United States have thought a great deal about representative and participatory political processes and, indeed, economic developmental processes. I am simply suggesting that, in dialogue with other countries, the United States should raise questions that come out of its knowledge of how that process applies to another country. I would not tell another country how it applies; I would simply raise the question.

AMBASSADOR BASHEER: Let me take a hypothetical issue. If, today, there is universal suffrage in, say, Saudi Arabia, and the people have an honest, one-person, one-vote system, and there is a democracy in Saudi Arabia, do you think your interests will be served that way?

MR. SAUNDERS: Not necessarily, and I would not propose to the government of Saudi Arabia that it adopt universal suffrage or any other form of electoral system. What I would do is raise the question. I do not mean only to Saudi Arabia in this case, but to any developing country, I would raise the question about how that country is going to deal with the fact that economic development encourages elements in the society that were previously outside the decision-making processes to demand a voice. The question is how a country within the framework of its own institutions can devise a way to broaden participation in the decision-making process through its political institutions. I would simply point to the problem and raise the question without trying to prescribe an answer. It is a question that we have thought about a great deal in this country. We have done a great deal of academic work on it, and it is a question that is perhaps only coming to the fore in countries elsewhere in the world. What strikes me in looking at many of these countries is that they do have institutions that lend themselves to solving this problem, not with Western political forms, but with their own forms. These could be developed and applied if the problem is recognized, but I would agree with you completely that the United States should not—as we thought of doing twenty years ago—prescribe solutions for the political, social, and economic evolution of these countries. I am talking about putting a question in the air at the highest level so that others will consider it before they have to consider it in the streets.

MR. BOLLING: I wondered whether you and David Newsom would be willing to pursue this thought on negotiated change just a little farther with regard to the current issue. Take the problem of Lebanon. Here is a country that is in total shambles. It is partly in a shambles because of the intervention of various other countries. You have made clear that you do not want to propose some sophomoric American intervention to give Lebanon a plan for solving it. I wonder if you would think a little farther with us as to what could be done in the way of raising the appropriate questions in the appropriate forums in which that issue might be considered. It does seem clear that part of the agony that is going on in that part of the world will not be solved until that country can once more find some formula for dealing with the problems and until its neighbors, particularly Syria and Israel, leave it alone for a while. The relationships between the Israelis and the Arabs will certainly not be furthered until something is done with that. Is that the kind of situation in which some negotiated change would have some meaning? We can look at the situation in Iran, we can look at the situation in Yemen, and so on; those are historical, but here we are faced with a real live situation right now. What could be done to promote negotiated change in the very limited sense in which it would be realistic and not a sophomoric dream?

MR. NEWSOM: I do not mean to debate the question, but I do think that Lebanon is a very special kind of problem. Harold Saunders is talking about countries in which the internal social structure, the distribution of wealth, the political institutions, come under the severe stress of new generations, of movements of population, of natural disasters, and/or of subversive outside intervention bringing about pressures for political change. Lebanon is not an internal Lebanese problem anymore; it is an international problem. An effort is being made to negotiate it now, albeit with some problems. I do not think it is an example of exactly the kind of social-economic-political pressures for internal change that we have been talking about.

JOSEPH J. SISCO, Sisco Associates: I wonder whether we can generalize on the basis of these several principles that you have indicated. The appropriate policy in Iran might very well have been to try to shore up the shah even at the late hour. I am not suggesting this, but in line with what you have termed supporting our friends, it might have been in our interests if we were smart enough to try to influence the Israeli election. I am not so sure that we could not have done so and that we could not have known what direction our influence would have taken. Let's take Saudi Arabia in the aftermath of the attack on the mosque. Our Saudi friends are very sensitive to internal developments. Perhaps we are not sensitive enough when we tend to overemphasize, as we do from time to time, the Soviet challenge. We have come to realize that the question of oil production, for example, is politically sensitive to Saudi Arabia. We have also realized that the Saudis cannot afford to allow their internal situation to go unattended; the attack on the mosque certainly was a warning sign. In that particular instance, it might have been in our interest to go well beyond merely pointing out to the Saudis at the highest level that they have to be sensitive to their internal situation. In the case of Lebanon, it might be in our interest ultimately to offer a full-blown plan for reconciling the differences between the right and the left, between the Muslims and the Christians, in order to try to put Humpty Dumpty back together again, not exactly as in the past, but with some semblance of what it looked like in the past.

Why have I cited these different examples? In listening to the principles, I wondered, as a policy maker, if one can be categoric in saying that in all instances we should limit ourselves merely to making the leadership sensitive to the country's internal situation. That is really not enough insofar as America's policy is concerned. I wonder how applicable can be the enunciation of what are essentially universal principles relating to the entire Middle East and the Persian Gulf.

MR. SAUNDERS: These three series of comments all weave together. There is no question that a set of principles will not apply universally in all cases. Policy is developed for particular relations with particular nations. We are not even going to do that, however, in Lebanon, or in Saudi Arabia, or in some other country unless the people at the top of our government say that it is a matter of American priority to do so. As you know better than most people in this room, it is all very well and good to think that this is a useful thing to do in the conversations within the State Department, but unless the president and the secretary of state think in aggressive terms like this, that this is something that ought to be on their agenda whenever they make a decision vis-à-vis a country, it is probably not going to happen. It will not become a part of our decision-making process. By addressing the subject and urging that the subject be made a matter of priority, I am simply trying to get it on the agenda, or on the mental agenda of the top decision makers.

MR. SISCO: Over the last twenty or thirty years, there have been periods when we have been overinvolved in the internal aspects. Perhaps other periods of our history have been characterized by a lack of involvement, by a lack of sensitivity, or by a lack of intervention. I use these words in the broadest sense. In the aftermath of Vietnam, we have been very reluctant and confined and sensitive to what we might consider to be involvement along these economic developmental lines. Other periods could be characterized as more interventionist. Where we are today, I do not really know. That evaluation must be made on a country-by-country basis.

MR. SAUNDERS: At the beginning of the 1960s, there was a burst of interventionist thinking on a broad scale. At the end of the Vietnam intervention and in the early 1970s there was, for other reasons, a tendency not to tell other countries how to manage their own affairs, and there was a withdrawal from that kind of involvement. But today, for two reasons, perhaps, it is a time for reassessing our posture on this point. We are getting through the post-Vietnam withdrawal period, and we are realizing that we do need, particularly in the Middle East, a more active degree of involvement. Furthermore, the pace and the nature of change in the Middle East has burst upon us in the last six or seven years and in some ways poses problems that we have never had to face before. It therefore requires a new quality of response.

LUKE BATTLE, School of Advanced International Studies, Johns Hopkins University: I am rather puzzled by two or three apparently related questions. I do not know where to draw the line, for example, between negotiated change and mediation and intervention. Looking back over the Middle East situation in the last years, I have been trying to find successes as well as failures, but there have clearly been more failures. There are one or two that could be called successful. The 1958 involvement in Lebanon lasted for quite a long time, and the U.S. involvement was successful for a long period of time. The mediation in Cyprus in 1967, which involved considerable internal problems for each of the countries involved, was generally successful. I have trouble understanding exactly how to draw this line.

Part of the question you raise with respect to Iran, and also with respect to Egypt, has to do with elements of timing. Certainly in

Iran, we were not at all reticent in trying to create social change over a long period of time, in land reforms, in women's rights, in a whole series of things. We may not have intervened or negotiated quickly enough on the problem that you and David Newsom were talking about, but it was not an absence of urging change or of trying to negotiate it. It was a question whether we interpreted adequately and quickly enough the switch within the country itself that made that change really necessary. That is where we failed. We were not reticent at all, however, about pressing social change on Egypt or about pressing for withdrawal from Yemen. So it seems to me that the line between military intervention, as in Lebanon and in other places, and mediation, as in Cyprus, is obscure. They are all elements of negotiating change that have an impact internally as well as externally.

MR. NEWSOM: There is one other thing that needs to be considered. That is the changes that have taken place in the area itself. The situation in which we worked in 1958 cannot be equated with the situation in which we have to work in 1980. The countries with which we are dealing are no longer in any real sense dependent on us, particularly Saudi Arabia, which is now clearly independent in wealth and in its politics. It has a new generation that has already strutted on the world stage and feels confident. It is much more difficult to convey the kind of advice, even if it were sought, that we might have conveyed twenty years ago. The whole idea of military intervention that made our negotiation in Lebanon in 1958 possible is no longer a viable option in internal matters in the Middle East. By the evolution of the petroleum dollars and of new generations, because of the proliferation of countries and because of the different atmosphere, the kind of experience that we had twenty years ago may no longer be applicable.

MR. SAUNDERS: That is precisely one of the points that I am making, that we do have such a markedly different situation, and we have immensely important interests. The question is how the United States plays a role in this process. I do not think we have the option of not relating to it in some way. The question is how to play the role. That returns us to drawing the line between negotiated change and mediation and various other forms of involvement. I used the phrase "negotiated change" in a rather general sense. I did not mean that the United States would participate in an across-the-table negotiation of a change situation. I think of the word "negotiated" to mean a change that is worked out peacefully among the elements of the indigenous body politic to produce a new situation that rids the country of some potentially destabilizing dissent. The United States might play a mediatory role in that situation. It is not at all impossible that the United States in some auxiliary or complementary role might facilitate exchanges among the parties in Lebanon to breed some new form of national consensus. We may well be moving in that direction, at the request of the parties involved. I see a variety of roles here. The question I am really addressing is whether we lean forward and look for opportunities of this kind and eagerly accept the requests when they come, or whether we hang back and not involve ourselves.

WOLF BLITZER, *Jerusalem Post*: The major opportunity that the United States has to negotiate changes in the Middle East is not so much to negotiate internal changes within countries per se but to negotiate changes between countries. Where the United States has demonstrated the political will to get involved in effecting changes between countries, there has been success. Obviously, the most remarkable success was the change that developed between Israel and Egypt as a result of the extensive U.S. involvement. Clearly, if we take a look at the progress in relations between Israel and Egypt since the 1973 war, it was for the most part the result of such a strong U.S. involvement. That change probably would not have developed without U.S. involvement. Moshe Dayan has always pointed out that the years of secret negotiations between Israel and Jordan failed to produce anything, while the above-board negotiations between Israel and Egypt succeeded primarily because of the U.S. factor. The United States was not involved in the behind-the-scenes discussions that took place between Israel and Jordan, but it was very much involved in the discussions between Israel and Egypt.

The changes that the United States can effect between countries could have a spill-over effect, influencing changes within a country. Obviously, the fact that Israel and Egypt have improved their relationship has an impact on what is going on in Egypt and what is going on in Israel. I would merely argue that you are right, that it is probably not very likely that the United States will create significant internal changes through a frontal attack to try to democratize or otherwise affect institutions within countries. When the United States does get involved in trying to effect changes between countries, there is a possibility for some dramatic results.

MR. SAUNDERS: It is certainly true that the international environment will affect stability in each of these countries. The unresolved Arab-

Israeli or Palestinian-Israeli conflicts are perfect cases in point. As we suggested, there is an interplay between that problem and the internal stability of some of these countries. The United States can play a role there.

I would suggest that there is another aspect of the international environment that I am talking about there today. The concept of what it takes to develop a nation and various strategies of economic development are parts of the international environment today. Ideas are carried to the capitals of these countries by American professors who sit with national planning commissions and by the World Bank and the International Monetary Fund. That is just as much a part of the international environment as the resolution of conflict between states, which is a very important thing.

JAMES CRITCHFIELD, Tetratech International: Two ingredients have not been mentioned today that I have over the years found increasingly important, and both of them lend themselves to negotiation. One is the question of the transfer of high technology, or just technology, and the other is the ability to negotiate with respect to resources. I have been increasingly impressed that probably no decision that a leader in a developing country makes is more important than the key issue of importing a certain kind of technology. Much of this is beyond his control. There is a certain dynamic quality to the world of technology, and there is no way he can stem it from flooding into his country. The leadership of a country also faces specific questions however, such as, do we build a steel mill; do we build a whole new infrastructure to develop an area for hydrocarbons or minerals; do we go for increasingly sophisticated weapon systems; do we go for a level of technology and agricultural development that may be a dramatic step forward from what we have traditionally done; do we develop national water supplies on the basis of technologies that are unknown to the country; do we get into the business of international airlines; do we get into the shipping business; how far do we go in attempting to play the game of keeping up with the industrial nations, not only in producing resources but in processing them. The head of a Middle Eastern country really has a two-phase decision to make when he considers importing an item of technology (and when I use that term, I mean the whole technology that is involved when an oil company comes in to develop a 10,000-square-mile area, to explore and then to develop the resources that are found). The first part of the decision is whether to import this technology. Immediately after that comes the much tougher question of whether to sacrifice efficiency by nationalizing the operation of the equipment or to be extremely efficient in the use of this technology and import foreign experts to make it work. Those two decisions have a huge cumulative impact on how they develop as nations.

Saudi Arabia is buying all the technology conceivably available. Iran was an even more advanced case of this. Some of the developing countries are beginning to worry about becoming the owners of a herd of white elephants, and they are slowing down development and being more circumspect in their decisions. We eventually come to such questions as, Should we and the Soviet Union negotiate a way to develop energy resources that will reduce the opportunity for conflict between the Soviet Union and the United States, because that conflict is the major concern of most of the countries in the whole Indian Ocean and Middle East region? Are the Americans and the Soviets, in this competition for resources, going to push into the region to a degree that will jeopardize the stability of this whole area?

All of this falls under the heading of what could be called opportunity through negotiations.

MR. SAUNDERS: I would add a third question to those that you say the leadership must consider, and that is, What will be the internal political consequences of these first two decisions of whether to import, whether to nationalize?

HERBERT STEIN, American Enterprise Institute: What puzzles me about your description of the role of the U.S. government in the management of change in the Middle East is that I do not see how you distinguish the role of the U.S. government from the role of the Brookings Institution or of the American Enterprise Institute or of Harvard University. If the whole function is to bring to bear the accumulated wisdom of American experts or bureaucrats, then the government of Saudi Arabia can hire American experts and bureaucrats just as good as those the State Department can hire. I would think that the difference between the U.S. government and the American Enterprise Institute is that the U.S. government has more power and more interest, but you seem to be exceedingly humble about the willingness to apply U.S. power or anything but suggestions arising out of our experience in observing history. Is that really what experts in this field have to tell us citizens of the United States?

MR. SAUNDERS: Let me make two comments; the second will lead into a follow-up to your point. The U.S. government has one ability that AEI, Brookings, and Harvard do not have; that is, it has the capacity in its talks with high-level political leaders in other countries to put something at the top of a worry list, a priority list, in a way that the academics never can. When the president of the United States says it seems worth worrying about this, that has an impact that no product of the academic or research community can have. It may be, however, that the research community has to bring the idea into its own time before the president of the United States will be moved to do that.

You asked how the United States should employ its power in this area, or are there not other ways in which we should employ our power. I am not sure that this is what you intended, but we must say a word about the role of American military power in this situation. You might elaborate on your meaning of power.

MR. STEIN: In the beginning you defined power to include economic power, political power—I suppose those are the main ingredients. Suppose it is something different.

MR. SAUNDERS: It is different to the extent that it implies action by governments and the recommendation or an urging or an enticement of the U.S. government to that kind of action. Let me go beyond your point, because we do have to say a word about military power in this connection. If another regime, or a regime in another country, is faced with the threat of overthrow because of a revolution, should the United States use or support the use of force to prevent that? Iran is the case in point. We have been told it is important for the United States to reestablish its credibility as a friend, to reestablish confidence that the United States will come to the aid of its friends if they are threatened. We have been told that the United States let the shah down and that that has harmed our credibility around the world. Our friends no longer believe that we will use our power to keep them in power. The question is, What is the role of American military power or, indeed, other military power in coping with the challenges to authority that grow out of the process of political, social, economic change?

MR. STEIN: I once sat next to Art Buchwald at a dinner, some years ago, when it had just been revealed that the United States had spent $7 million to get rid of Chilean dictator Salvador Allende. Buchwald observed that that was a terrible thing to do, at the same time that we were pursuing détente with the Soviet Union. I asked whether he thought if we could have gotten rid of Brezhnev for $7 million, we would not have done it. That is an example of influencing the internal behavior of a country by providing arms to a friendly government or a government that we think is on our side as against internal opposition. Those seem to be the normal incidents of statecraft in this world. Is that ruled out in your view of the situation, or is there something special about the Middle East?

MR. SAUNDERS: A military relationship with a friendly regime is not at all ruled out. It is part of the normal relationships that we have and part of enhancing the authority of friendly regimes. The question really is, At the moment its authority is questioned by the people of a country, what is the role of military force, either theirs or ours?

I would question whether there is a situation like that in which the United States could effectively intervene. That is an assertion open to challenge, and it does have, as someone said earlier, a lot to do with the timing of the action when it comes to the use by indigenous governments of their own military authority to bring the course of the revolution under control.

# 3

# The Soviet Threat in the Middle East: What Is It?

A Conversation with Harold H. Saunders

*July 7, 1981*

In our previous conversations I made several points that set the stage for today's discussion about the place of the Middle East and Southwest Asia in the global strategic context. I began by noting that it has long been a strategic interest of the United States to prevent Soviet predominance in this area and to avoid the confrontation between the United States and the Soviet Union that would result from a Soviet effort to achieve predominance there. In the 1980s, apart from the independent development of American and Soviet military power and barring a major reorientation in Eastern Europe, this volatile area could well be the principal area for shaping the global balance of power in the 1990s.

The past security system in this area has broken down on two levels. First, the system built in the 1950s around the northern tier states—Turkey, Iran, Pakistan, and at that time Iraq, with British and American collaboration—began to fade in the 1960s and then ended in name as well in 1978–1979 with the withdrawal of Iran. Turkey, of course, remains part of NATO. Even in the 1950s, however, the Soviet Union leapfrogged the northern tier by establishing a close military supply and economic assistance relationship with Egypt and some of the other Arab countries. Today there is no clear East-West line in the Middle East and Southwest Asia. Not only is there no geographic line, but there is no clear delineation of our respective legitimate interests and presences in the area.

More immediately, the security system in the Persian Gulf, which had developed there after the British retrenchment at the end of 1970, collapsed with the Iranian revolution in 1978–1979. Through the 1970s, the United States had decided to rest the security system there on the collaboration between Iran and Saudi Arabia, relying most heavily on Iranian military strength and continuing American military supply relationships with both countries. With the revolution in Iran, Iran not only ceased to be an active partner in that system but became a potential source of instability as the countries of the Gulf began to fear export of the Iranian revolution through the Shiite minorities on the western side of the Gulf.

The Soviet invasion of Afghanistan in this context raised the threat of direct Soviet military intervention in this area in a way that we had not had to deal with since the late 1940s and early 1950s, with the unique exceptions of Soviet threats to take military action during the Arab-Israeli wars of 1956, 1967, and 1973. The disintegration of central authority in Iran opened the possibility of a Soviet military move into one of the Iranian provinces, either in direct aggression or in nominal support of some regime declaring local autonomy. Beyond that, it was logical to assume that the Soviets would at least be preparing contingency plans for moving a large Soviet force to the shores of the Persian Gulf and beyond. Soviet imperial aspirations seemed to threaten the free world's lifeblood in this area in a way that we had not experienced in some three decades—just at a time when the energy crunch was moving toward its peak.

Since Southwest Asia is literally vital to our allies in Europe and Japan because of its oil, the new situation there and the new Soviet moves there have made this a central subject of discussion in the various forums of our alliances. We have found not only that there is a strong common interest in preserving the independence and stability of the key nations in this area but that our differing perspectives and responsibilities sharply increase the likelihood of severe divisions among us over what should be done in this area. The 1973 Arab-Israeli war and oil embargo showed that tension in the Middle East has the capability to drive a wedge between the United States and its allies. The fact remains that the shift of focus in the global contest to Southwest Asia makes this a critical subject in determining how the Western and Japanese alliances will develop.

Against that background, a new security system will have to emerge in this central area. That new system will have two requirements. First, it will require the strengthening of the key countries in the area to resist external attack and internal subversion. It will also require the evolution of relationships among the key countries in the area for cooperation in maintaining the independence of the area. Second, it will require a relationship between the United States and the Soviet Union that will avoid confrontation there while blocking further Soviet aggression. A part of this requirement is greater clarity about the readiness of the United States to support the independence of these nations, particularly to define exactly what the U.S. security position and military readiness should be. Most people in Washington today agree that it is important that adversaries see U.S. military power as a believable threat and that friends believe we will use it in their support. There has been much talk about restoring our credibility in this area, but there remains great uncertainty and sharp disagreement as to how our military power might be used.

In discussing the challenge to our interests of accelerating social, political, and economic change in this area, I noted that the Soviets have most commonly achieved a degree of influence that prevents indigenous leadership from independently making its final decisions by working politically through the internal social and political dynamics of these nations. While the threat of direct total administrative and military takeover on the Afghan model is a threat that cannot be ignored, concentrating on that threat as the most likely danger risks overlooking the broader techniques by which the Soviets have increased their influence. If our interest precisely defined lies in the independence of indigenous leadership to make its own final decisions, such as where to sell oil, how to relate to neighbors and other powers, and how to use their military forces, it would seem to be worth a good deal more effort than we have expended to understand what makes countries vulnerable or resistant to this kind of Soviet influence. It is also important to recognize that as long as indigenous leadership retains the capacity to assess its own interests and makes its own decisions, the problems we have to deal with in our relationships with them are not all made in Moscow; they are a combination of local forces plus Soviet and Western influence.

### The Issues Posed

The issues posed for discussion today are these:

- How exactly should we define the Soviet threat? What exactly concerns us about the Soviet presence in this area and what real limits do we seek to impose on it?
- What should be our strategy in dealing with the Soviet threat to this area? What is our appropriate military policy? Should we try to negotiate an understanding with the U.S.S.R.? How should

we deal with our allies in approaching this area? What relationships should we establish between ourselves and key countries in the Middle East? What relationships should we encourage among those countries to blunt the Soviet thrust? Do we have any further wisdom about our own approach to the question of encouraging orderly rather than disruptive change in this area?

Let me talk a bit about each of these issues before we turn to discussion.

## The Nature of the Soviet Threat

Many conversations between our top political leaders and those in the Middle East begin with a discussion of the strategic threat. Such discussions start from the premise that the ultimate Soviet objective is to gain a controlling grip on key points that will dominate the sea lanes and flow of vital oil to the industrialized world.

In the East, the Pakistanis and the Iranians have long feared that the Soviet objective was to establish a corridor through Baluchistan for direct access to the Indian Ocean. The Soviet invasion of Afghanistan has further encouraged these fears and has brought Soviet military forces to the borders of Pakistan itself.

Some Iranians even today express concern that the Soviets might either set up a puppet regime in Azerbaijan or Khuzistan and establish a Soviet military presence there poised to move to the oil centers of the Gulf.

The Saudis are also concerned over those possibilities. They have further expressed their fear of Soviet support for subversive forces working in the Gulf. They have seen the close Soviet military supply and treaty relationships with Iraq as Soviet collaboration with a radical regime, which, for its own purposes, has sought to undermine traditional regimes in the Arabian Peninsula and in the Gulf and to establish itself as the predominant influence in that area.

They have also watched with concern the large Soviet diplomatic presence in Kuwait. They have seen Soviet support for nationalist movements such as the Palestine Liberation Organization as another point of entry for the Soviets in the area. They have seen the unresolved Arab-Israeli conflict as a principal opportunity for the Soviets to spread their presence in the area. The Saudis have also continuously underscored their concern for the strengthening of the Soviet military and political position in South Yemen and across the straits in the horn of Africa. They have pressed us hard to aid Somalia and the Sudan to resist Soviet, East European, and Cuban gains in both those areas.

President Sadat would share the concerns expressed by his neighbors to the east and voice a particular added concern for the area immediately surrounding Egypt. His military advisers point to the large buildup of Soviet equipment in neighboring Libya and to Libyan expeditions into Chad and subversion in other parts of Africa. The Egyptians have also formed a close relationship with the Sudan to protect their own vital flow of water from the headwaters of the Nile. They have urged U.S. assistance both to the Sudan and to Somalia.

Moving briefly even farther to the west, the Tunisians and Moroccans both would point to the Libyan threat and to their concern about the Soviet strategic presence in the Mediterranean.

The Israelis have over the years fluctuated in the intensity of their concentration on the Soviet threat. They have normally taken the posture that it is a U.S. responsibility to deal with what they have often called the "outer ring," meaning the Soviet threat in the area. At the same time, they have accepted responsibility for protecting their own borders. At times when the Israelis have felt the need for increased U.S. military supply or support for Israel's diplomatic positions, the Israelis have emphasized the immediacy of the Soviet threat. At other times, when they feared that excessive American concern would translate itself into pressure on Israel to move toward an Arab-Israeli settlement at a pace that made them uncomfortable, they have deemphasized the immediacy of the Soviet threat. Underlying their approach to the United States has been the view that Israel must be seen in the United States as a strategic asset in the U.S. contest with the Soviet Union.

Americans have not generally differed with this larger picture of the threat, but there have been differences over exactly how to analyze and to deal with it. Whereas our friends in the region have normally stressed the importance of greater military support to countries resisting Soviet-supported forces, the United States has taken the somewhat broader view of emphasizing that the Soviet threat is not strictly a military problem and that strengthening internal forces against the causes of instability and revolution is perhaps an even stronger bulwark against Soviet expansion. Part of this position stems from a genuine American feeling that the Soviet thrust is much broader than simply a military threat and that local governments have a responsibility to man the first line of defense by tending to their own stability. This position is also partly the result of inability to provide financial and security assistance on a scale desired by our friends.

In analyzing the Soviet threat, the United States has identified a wide range of elements. Marxist-Leninist analysis, vocabulary, and political action techniques have provided the basis of a relationship, as in Afghanistan, between Moscow and local revolutionaries with their own indigenous agendas and unique characteristics. The Soviets also contribute a steady stream of international propaganda against what they call reactionary regimes.

Moscow has taken advantage of revolutionary situations, such as that in South Yemen in the 1960s or Iran in 1978–1979, to strengthen local Communist parties. It attempts to improve their credentials through the classic policy of aligning themselves with the revolutionary movement and positioning themselves for a takeover at a later stage.

Military supply and substantial economic assistance have been major vehicles for the Soviets in broadening their presence. In some cases, such as Egypt in an earlier period, South Yemen, Iraq, Syria, and Libya, Soviet military equipment has been accompanied by a substantial number of Soviet advisers. In some of these countries the Soviets have even gone beyond that point to negotiate access to facilities for their own naval and other forces.

The Soviet administrative and military presence in Afghanistan is, so far, unique in the Middle East and Southwest Asia, but it raises the concern about the existence of Soviet plans for a direct military move to the Persian Gulf.

In the diplomatic sphere, the Soviets have used the instrument of the friendship treaty to develop relationships at varying periods in Ethiopia, Egypt, South Yemen, Syria, Iraq, Afghanistan, and India. These treaties actually only commit the two sides to consultations and are subject to the policies of the participating governments at the moment. They have, however, given the Soviets the appearance of establishing a more formal presence in key countries in the area, and they have provided a framework for military collaboration.

More generally, the Soviets have moved on the global stage to achieve some degree of legitimacy for their position in the area. Their cochairmanship of the Geneva Middle East Conference in December 1973 was one example of their recognition as a legitimate participant in helping to establish a peaceful order in this area. Since their exclusion from the peace process beginning in 1974, they have repeatedly called for a return to Geneva or for an international conference of Arab-Israeli settlement to reestablish themselves as a full participant in the process of arbitrating the future of the area.

## Elements of a U.S. Response

In the light of this analysis of the Soviet threat, what can we say about the limits we would like to impose on the Soviet presence in the Middle East and Southwest Asia and about our strategy for achieving those objectives?

First, we need to give higher priority in our bilateral relations to dealing with the forces of political and social change. U.S. interests are harmed when governments come to power, as in Afghanistan, that are either so dominated by Moscow that they are not free to make their own decisions or so hostile to the United States ideologically, as in Iran, that the United States cannot establish a working relationship. In the strategic context it is essential to make a distinction between that situation, as in Afghanistan, where a direct breach of independence has taken place and the situation, as in Iran or other nations, where Soviet-supported parties are competing for dominance. In the extreme case of Soviet takeover, the issue is with Moscow. In the case where Soviet-supported parties are competing for power, the issue is how that competition will come out.

This is not a new question, but it is one that has not been high on the policy maker's agenda in the recent past. In dealing with the threat of Soviet subversion, we need in the first instance to analyze and to address internal issues that the Soviets and radical domestic forces can exploit. We still have actively before us the question we discussed in our last session—how the United States can identify and can deal with the causes of internal instability while still not involving itself unacceptably in the internal affairs of other countries. One aspect of a response is adopting a posture that encourages governmental effectiveness, leadership, and responsiveness. Another is providing help to governments in enhancing their own internal security. In doing so, the United States must accept and minimize the risk that it may be overly identified with repressive regimes rather than with the reasonable forces for orderly change. We can become a part of the problem if we do not use our involvement with internal security to encourage responsiveness to legitimate pressures for change.

Second, in blunting both subversion and external aggression, we must decide how to relate to cooperation within the region on internal and external security matters. There is cooperation among some groups of states in the area on this issue. The question is whether the United States should relate to those groups in any way other than through normal bilateral cooperation. While it is clear that they will want to develop their own organization without any kind of U.S. involvement, the question is whether eventually there will be a possibility of cooperation among like-minded states, including Israel, in the context of an Arab-Israeli settlement. It is too soon to propose that now, but it is an issue that is already in some minds and must be left on the agenda for the more distant future. Meanwhile, the United States needs a strategic vision of how it will develop its cooperative relationship in a way that is consistent with the strategy of preventing Soviet gains in the area.

Third, a critical issue is whether and, if so, how the United States should use elements of its military power. The military strategy of the United States toward this region reaches back over the years to World War II, but President Carter's statement in his January 23, 1980, State of the Union address broke new ground in stating our policy toward the Persian Gulf region. He said: "An attempt by any outside force to gain control of the Persian Gulf region will be regarded as an assault on the vital interests of the United States of America, and such an assault will be repelled by any means necessary, including military force." Those officials within the Carter administration charged with implementing this commitment will be among the first to recognize that this statement was the beginning and not the culmination of a process of thinking through exactly what our military commitments in the area are and what kind of resources need to be committed to fulfill those promises. Recent articles by former Under Secretary of State David Newsom and former Ambassador Chris Van Hollen are two of the articulate statements that identify issues yet to be addressed. These issues fall into three major areas.

The initial question is what kind of military force the United States should develop to meet contingencies in this area. The U.S. government recognized the need to improve its capability to project military force into this area. The Rapid Deployment Force became the focal point of efforts to improve that capability, and we negotiated with governments in the area for use of support facilities that would be necessary if larger American forces were to be deployed into the area. Meanwhile, the U.S. naval buildup in the Indian Ocean was already an accomplished fact.

The related question revolves around the issue of how such a force would be used. Vis-à-vis the Soviet Union, military and political planners alike had to cope with the reality that the United States is unlikely ever to be able to project forces into this area on a large enough scale to confront decisively the number of divisions the Soviets can move across their own borders into the area. This reality leads to the need among the strategists for a policy such as the "tripwire" strategy employed in Western Europe, which would enable the United States to make use of a modestly effective force as a signal to the Soviets that a military clash in Southwest Asia could lead to a broader conflict.

Vis-à-vis internal stability, planners had to confront the issue of responding to the concern of moderate regimes about what they can count on from the United States if they are challenged as the shah was. Are U.S. forces being designed to protect regimes from internal challenge or to protect the independence and integrity of nations from external attack?

Our military strategy toward the area encompasses our military supply relations and the degree to which we rely on local forces to defend their own nations before the United States considers its own action. Repeated questions are raised in Washington about what should be our military supply relationship with Israel, Jordan, Saudi Arabia, Egypt, and Pakistan. Without a clear-cut strategy toward the role of indigenous forces, the administration and the Congress become engaged in a sharp debate every time major military sales are proposed. Enhancing the defensive capability of friendly states in the area is clearly a part of enhancing the stability of the area, and yet each major sale leads to deep divisions within the American body politic.

Until these questions are thought through, we can go on in the near future to develop the Rapid Deployment Force, but at some point soon, we will need to define more clearly what its eventual size, capability, and purposes should be.

Fourth, on the diplomatic front, the United States faces a profound choice between two possible approaches to dealing with the Soviet Union. The first approach would be to work out with the Soviets, through a process of discussion and negotiation, a series of understandings that would define the interests of each party in this area and the limits of each side's tolerance for the other's role. In the past, some moves were made in this direction. For instance, talks were proposed about the limitation of naval forces in the Indian Ocean; we also engaged in negotiations about the terms for an Arab-Israeli settlement. In 1973, we even cochaired the Middle East peace conference at Geneva. Most recently, discussions have been proposed leading toward Soviet withdrawal from Afghanistan. To take this approach is not necessarily to reach some sort of overarching agreement that would divide the Middle East between us; that would not be acceptable to the parties in the area. It does suggest, however, a greater understanding about what each of us is trying to do in the area and about what kind of presence each considers essential. In deciding to try this approach again, the United States would have to be prepared in advance to cope with the deep suspicion of friends in the region that the superpowers were getting together at their expense.

The alternative approach is that each of us would establish our positions in the area through continuing competition. This is essentially the approach that we have adopted since 1973–1974. In taking this approach, the United States has taken a central role in moving the Arab-Israeli conflict through a series of partial agreements. Since 1979, we have been developing our own military capability in response to the disintegration of central authority in Iran and to the Soviet invasion of Afghanistan. As long as the Soviets remain in Afghanistan and refuse to negotiate a settlement that would lead to their withdrawal, the U.S. government has felt it would be difficult to conceive a negotiation or a series of negotiations with the Soviets in this area. It has, therefore, continued to build its own presence with the thought that the Soviets ultimately would have to accommodate to it.

Fifth, as a complement to the way we deal directly with the Soviet Union in this area, we must also develop a strategy for collaboration with our European and Japanese allies. An excellent report submitted to the Trilateral Commission by four authors from Europe, Japan, and the United States, including former Under Secretary of State Joseph J. Sisco, put this problem in perspective.

> The strategy to be followed by the Trilateral regions in the Middle East cannot be less complex than the strategy which, in the 1950s and 1960s, succeeded in stabilising power relations in Europe and in opening the road to a period of coexistence and détente. . . . The problems of the Middle East, although they now appear to us to be uniquely dangerous, are certainly not more so than the problems which the industrialized democracies faced in the first two post-war decades. They are to some extent new problems, and we may still lack some of the knowledge needed to devise and carry out a complex strategy—a strategy whose aim must be to strengthen the independent political structures of the Middle East and to organise a credible response to the Soviet challenge, while bringing back to life the policy of co-existence and cooperative relations. The actors in this new international game are many, and they cannot and should not be manipulated by the power of the Trilateral regions. Many creative efforts were required in order to set up the great international institutions of this era. They were the creation of the political vision of statesmen. Such vision

is equally needed today if we want to avoid the risk that a strategy of expansion in the Middle East should become 'compellingly attractive even to a relatively prudent [Soviet] leadership.' Only a credible and determined Trilateral presence and policy today can avoid future fatal choices between war and surrender.

Sixth, the overarching question that needs to be dealt with is whether we need to design a military strategy for blocking direct Soviet military aggression toward the Persian Gulf or a political-military strategy for the entire Middle East and Southwest Asia area. Are we still going to try, as we did in the 1970s, to deal separately with the Persian Gulf and with the Arab-Israeli areas? Can we have a policy for blocking further extension of Soviet control in this area without paying as much attention to our efforts to reduce the causes of conflict in the area as we pay to strengthening our own military capability? Would U.S. military preparedness have prevented the Soviet position in South Yemen? Could it have prevented the Soviet invasion of Afghanistan? If so, how?

My own thesis throughout these conversations has been that we can no longer deal with the Middle East problem piecemeal in the 1980s, that we need a strategy that encompasses the full range of American interests in this area, and that we need to employ the full range of diplomatic, political, economic, and military assets. That assertion still needs to be examined and challenged.

I start from the twin premises that the threat is more than just Soviet military aggression and that the United States will not have the capability soon, if ever, by itself to defeat the Soviet Union militarily on this ground. If those premises are correct, the question is whether it is possible to put together a multilateral strategy with separate elements that will be strong enough to sustain our position in this area.

### Issues for Discussion

In light of this analysis of the challenge and the opportunities in this area, I suggest that we now turn to our discussion and concentrate on the following issues:

- What limits do we want to impose on the Soviet presence in this area?
- What military capability should we build and what should we expect it to achieve?
- How would we use our military forces in situations other than meeting direct Soviet military invasion?

- Should we move toward a series of discussions and negotiations with the Soviet Union to establish limits for the American and Soviet presence and activities in this area? Or should we attempt to establish them through a continuing competition between us in the area?
- Finally, are we kidding ourselves to think that any strategy that does not include the ability to defeat the Soviet Union on the ground can succeed?

## QUESTIONS AND ANSWERS

WILLIAM HYLAND, Carnegie Endowment for International Peace: In your choices of whether we should have a limited strategy of dealing only with the Soviets and blocking them from the Persian Gulf or should have a broader strategy, obviously your preference, and ours, is the broader strategy. The problem is that the Soviet threat, as someone said at the very outset, is kind of a moveable feast. Iran was quite a surprise to the Soviets. It was something that they worried about and then considered more favorably and then worried about again and now are back to thinking it may be a favorable turn for them. I personally was rather surprised how easily the Soviets were able to shift from Iraq to Iran even at a time when Iraq could have used a substantial amount of Soviet support. The Soviets also blatantly signed the treaty with Syria when Iraq supposedly was still an ally. All this suggests a fairly obvious point, which is that Soviet policy is quite fluid. The Soviets are looking around for a kind of magic combination of Iran, Syria, Libya, South Yemen, perhaps as a base in an area in which they suddenly have a great deal more interest. In the middle or late 1970s, they felt that they had been frozen out and that they were rapidly losing ground. Now they see the possibility for a substantial comeback, and this is not directly a result of Afghanistan. Afghanistan tends to be in their view a separate problem. It is not negotiable, regardless of what Lord Carrington may think. The Soviets are not going to negotiate their way out of Afghanistan. I do not think it cost them as much as many others think. For them it is a tolerable price, in that they are in Afghanistan to stay. It gives them tremendous leverage, but I have no clear picture of where they go from there. The rest of the combinations depend greatly on Iran. In Soviet policy it is Iran that is the big question mark, but if they could establish an influence and a presence in Iran, that would be a substantial leap forward that would make up for all of the Egyptian expulsions and other setbacks.

That is where the United States erred, in my view. The rest of the policy does not bother me as much as it does the experts. I found the Carter doctrine not so bad; I found what has been done in rapid deployment not so bad. What I do not understand is how we intend to work with or around the revolution in Iran. Iran is still an enormously powerful country. The Soviets have focused a lot of attention and effort there. If they get a foothold of some kind in Iran, we are in very big trouble.

That raises an issue you swept aside a little too quickly. Maybe we can negotiate with the Soviet Union, not about Afghanistan, but perhaps we could have some discussion about what happened to the rest of the area. Maybe we could even pick up some of the points it has been making about guarantees. That might not be the worst outcome for us or Iran; if we could get some kind of guarantee that it would be a neutral buffer zone, we might be well ahead of the game.

MR. SAUNDERS: May I ask you, as a Soviet specialist, to respond on one other point? If the so-called tripwire strategy, whatever that may have meant in Europe, is applied in this area, how seriously would the Soviets take an American capability to put some elements of a rapid deployment force on the ground in Iran, for instance, that the Soviets might bump into if they moved in that direction? How seriously would they take the threat that a clash with American soldiers, however small the force might be, would trigger some kind of larger confrontation? Is that something that they would be deeply concerned about, or would they feel that that was an inadequate force and that the United States would not really do anything else? How would the tripwire strategy operate in this case?

MR. HYLAND: The Soviets would always take the presence of American ground forces very seriously. Whenever they start killing American soldiers, even on a small scale, that is very serious, very dangerous. Air Force–Navy might be a little different, but in general the Soviets regard American military forces as a significant barrier, even in very small numbers. That is more a psychological and political deterrent than a military response. If the Soviet Union for some reason feels that it has to go into Pakistan, let us say to protect its investment in Afghanistan, it might feel that that is a vital interest of the Soviet Union and that even an American tripwire is not going to matter. In general, however, the American tripwire, while dangerous for us, is a substantial deterrent.

MR. SAUNDERS: What would happen if they tripped over the wire?

MR. HYLAND: The same thing that happened in Korea. We would pile in more and more troops, more and more resources. We would escalate, and they could never be totally positive that we would not use nuclear weapons.

MR. NEWSOM: I agree with Bill Hyland. We need to know more about Soviet intentions. There are some curious things about the current posture of the Soviets; it would be interesting to have Bill Hyland's reaction to this. At the time I left the government, there was no indication that the Soviets were preparing their deployment or the configuration of their forces in Afghanistan for any move beyond Afghanistan. Until the end of February, the Soviets gave the appearance of being very cautious about any provocative confrontations with Pakistan. Although they made some rhetorical assaults on Pakistan, they seemed to be, and as far as I know still are, making a meticulous effort to avoid a problem with Pakistan. We need to keep in mind that, although the Soviets have a strong military relationship with and a degree of influence in Syria, they cannot be said to be in control of Syria to the same extent, perhaps, that they are in control of the People's Democratic Republic of Yemen. Except in Afghanistan, the Soviets have not made a substantial gain in the Middle East since their departure from Egypt. Sometimes, in our occasional facile discussion of this issue, we give the impression that the Soviets are very much on the march in an area where, for some strange reason, they may even be showing some restraint. Certainly in Iran they do not seem to be making great headway. In spite of Ayatollah Khomeini's charges about American involvement in the bombing, the leftists there seem to be getting their heads cut off.

My impression has always been that if we placed ground forces in southern Iran, for example, the Soviets would feel that the treaty of 1921 gave them an international basis for moving into northern Iran. Even though the Iranians have said that they have abrogated the treaty, the Soviets have not.

MR. HYLAND: My impression is that what the Soviets would settle for, what they want, is not to march into these places, and I do not detect that kind of activity either. They would like to neutralize them as the first major step toward political change for the area; to make

Pakistan a neutral state, Afghanistan a buffer state, and Iran a non-aligned neutral state linked to Libya or Syria or a more radical regime. They would consider this a major geopolitical advance if it could be worked out without using any Soviet troops.

If the United States puts ground forces in southern Iran, it is inevitable that the Soviets will put ground forces in northern Iran. In fact, it would almost be an invitation. I can almost see the Soviet marshals saying that that is great, that is what Russia tried to do for a few hundred years—partition Iran and get their own sphere of influence nailed down with a great power agreement. It would be more effective to have American ground forces within striking distance of this area, reinforced by a policy that the United States would not stand idly by if the Soviet Union began to take advantage. The idea of putting American ground forces in southern Iran strikes me as total insanity as a first step.

MR. SAUNDERS: If one concludes that the Iranian revolution has accomplished the neutralization of Iran without any Soviet involvement, despite the former presence of the United States, how can Iran close the door to further Soviet advance?

CHRIS VAN HOLLEN, Carnegie Endowment for International Peace: I would like to follow up on some of the themes that have been struck by David Newsom and Bill Hyland. The whole question of Soviet interests and Soviet motivations is 'critical to a formulation of U.S. policy. Over the last two or three years, our policy has been driven by assumptions about Soviet interests and Soviet aspirations that may not be warranted by careful and close analysis. We also tend to intermix aspects of the Iranian revolution, particularly the hostage issue and the Soviet invasion of Afghanistan, in our ideas and approach. It is worth remembering, for example, that the initial search for facilities in Oman, in Somalia, and in Kenya had nothing to do with the Soviet movement in Afghanistan. The first State Department mission to the area returned before late December 1979. That initial search was on the subject of the seizure of hostages at the American embassy in Tehran rather than on the Soviet move into Afghanistan. There has been a tendency to meld the two and to see our strategy as based on the belief that the Soviet move into Afghanistan was simply the staging area for the move toward the Gulf or the warm water areas of the Indian Ocean. If our policy and approach is based on that assumption, then the disposition of our naval forces in the region and the entire aspect of the U.S. military buildup is governed by that consideration. Whether or not that is, in fact, the basic threat to American interests is something that we have passed over and not examined closely enough.

The whole issue of the movement of the region toward independence and nonalignment deserves closer examination. In fact, the moves in this direction could serve U.S. history. Bill Hyland concluded that an arrangement whereby Iran would be a buffer between the United States and the Soviet Union might ultimately serve American interests. I agree that indeed it might in the future. We might want to examine that as a possibility, at least.

As far as Iran is concerned, the centrality of the hostage issue over such an extended period and the continued attacks on the United States as the great Satan have obscured the militant nonalignment, and I underscore the word "nonalignment," that Iran has been practicing. Shortly after Khomeini came to power, Iran denounced the 1921 treaty with the Soviet Union. The Iranians must have infuriated the Soviets at the Second Islamic Conference in Islamabad when they included Afghan nationalists in the Iranian delegation. As far as I know, natural gas sales to the Soviet Union are still in abeyance, and the Soviet diplomatic mission in Iran remains sharply cut. There has been a militancy in the East-West context that sometimes is lost sight of; it may, depending on circumstances, serve American interests over time.

At the same time, the question of whether the Soviets have gained or lost in the Middle East often obscures the extraordinary change that has taken place in the Soviet-Iraqi relationship in a short time. While one may talk about the new treaty with Syria and the facility with which the Soviets signed with the Syrians, the question is whether that effectively compensates for the type of relationship that they developed with Iraq between 1972 and 1978.

In the case of Pakistan, it is interesting that even though the Pakistanis ultimately were willing to accept the deal offered by Washington—$3 billion over five years—they have bent over backwards to make it clear that this new military supply relationship with Pakistan is not in any way degrading to Pakistan's nonalignment or to its position in the Islamic world. This reflects the extraordinary evolution in Pakistani policy, which, when combined with the changes in Iran and Iraq and the adjustments in Saudi policy, indicates an entirely new political environment in the region. That climate may or may not significantly advance Soviet interests. The rocky relationship is certainly a setback to the Soviets. They probably felt much more comfortable in dealing with the shah than they do with the Khomeini regime.

A failure of the Carter administration and the continuing failure of the Reagan administration is to stand back and avoid really going through the fundamentals of U.S. interests in the region, the real threat to those interests, and the best way to design our policies across the board to meet those threats. Instead, we are dealing with decisions made in the heat of the moment about Iran and the hostage crisis, reinforced by the Soviet move into Afghanistan. Perhaps this is the time to stand back and take another look.

MR. BOLLING: If we are concerned about the question of Soviet penetration of the region, we cannot ignore, in relation to military matters, the question of political subversion in the area and the impact that has on the security problem. One thing that concerns many Arabs is that American policy and Israeli policy play into the hands of the most hostile elements within the Palestinian community and tend to subvert those who want to work toward a practical political solution. It is important to recognize that among the most pro-Western, pro-American, reconciliation-minded West Bank Palestinians, there is a strong conviction that it is the deliberate policy of the Israeli government to try to polarize the situation by giving covert encouragement to the most extremist elements among the West Bank Palestinians. The point of the policy is to give the impression that these elements speak for the Palestinians. I know very well one Christian family in Ramallah whose credentials are beyond question as far as their pro-Western point of view is concerned. One of them is a woman who is a leader in the Christian community among the Palestinians and who says that she is quite convinced that it is more difficult for her and for women's religious groups to have free speech and free assembly in the West Bank than it is for pro-Communist political groups, which seem to have the covert blessing of the Israeli government. They point to the fact that the Raka, the legal Marxist party within Israel, has strong links with the Communist elements in the West Bank. Those elements are allowed to hold their meetings. The two most radical mayors—Khalaf and Shaka—are allowed to continue to function as mayors, whereas much more moderate men, such as Milhelm and Kawasmeh, also from the West Bank, have been expelled. These are cited as illustrations of a concern that is widespread in moderate circles within the Arab countries, particularly among the Palestinians, both under Israeli occupation and outside of Israel, that there is a polarization, that there is a subversion of moderate Palestinians that plays into the hands of the Soviets again and again.

That brings me back to what must be dealt with ultimately, and that is whatever may be the soundest military policy in building

70

defenses against possible Soviet aggression. It could well be that our weakest point of defense is our inability to deal with the political problems relating to the Palestinians.

MR. SAUNDERS: Let's broaden that a bit. I will ask some of you who have spent your lives in the region to discuss this. What are your observations about the Soviet relationship with indigenous political parties and forces? Landrum Bolling mentioned one situation; David Newsom alluded to another situation that evolved in South Yemen, where, over the years, the Marxist party has gradually come to the top and is now in close relationship with the Soviet Union. In Afghanistan, the Marxist party first engaged in a coup and then, of course, ultimately came out on top.

What would those of you who are regional specialists like to observe about these leftist political parties, the Soviet relation to them, and the ability of moderate forces to prevent a recurrence of what happened in South Yemen or in Afghanistan?

MR. CRITCHFIELD: Much of this discussion falls within a broad framework with which probably everyone in the room has labored. At the beginning of the century, that part of the world was clearly defined as a British sphere of influence, extending from the Dardanelles to Tibet. That did not really change until the Russian Revolution. Between 1909 and 1918, there were tsarist and later Bolshevik forces briefly in Azerbaijan, on the Iranian littoral of the Caspian Sea, and in the Caucasus, but these withdrew under pressure. Then there was no longer a British sphere of influence, but an Anglo-American sphere of influence that extended along this same line. The Soviet and Anglo-American spheres of influence remained more or less identified on a single geographical line where they met. In the last ten or fifteen years, the Anglo-American sphere of influence first eroded, then disappeared, the last vestiges of it in the late 1970s. A map today would show a line from somewhere near Somalia just offshore along the Indian Ocean littoral, leaving the entire area of the Arabian Peninsula, Iran, Pakistan, India, in a no man's land that is not an American, nor a British, nor a Soviet sphere of influence today. Probably the only legitimate exception to that is the Soviet position in Afghanistan. I personally would say that Afghanistan has become part of a Soviet sphere of influence, and that that is quite consistent with the traditional cautious extension in which the Soviets have indulged for more than a century.

A large number of nations with which we have had relationships find their security today in this no man's land. The Soviet sphere of influence is still removed, mostly north of the historical Soviet border with these nations. The safety of traditional arrangements, however, is also gone.

What exists in the area now is a contest in which various countries, including the United States and the Soviet Union, have managed to establish something that we all describe as "presence." A presence is something less than a sphere of influence. It comprises psychological elements, troops, aid, and trade. It is doubtful that even South Yemen or Ethiopia, particularly because they are not contiguous to the Soviet Union, can really be described as part of a Soviet sphere. There are no recognizable lines, such as there are between the Warsaw Pact and the NATO countries.

The situation is ephemeral, and the individual countries are trying to find a formula for seeking their own security. All of them have adopted a new meaning for nonalignment, and it is genuine. It is not the label that was used in the 1950s and 1960s. They feel happiest when the Soviet forces remain north of the traditional line of Soviet influence and the Americans remain withdrawn to their new line somewhere south of the Strait of Hormuz and the Indian Ocean. The American sphere of influence ends with the naval presence in the Indian Ocean. All these countries are striving to find a formula in which they can live with nonalignment. It will be a formula that guarantees that superpower rivalry will somehow be kept north of the border of that part of the world and over the horizon. Within this formula, they are all seeking security. The rivalry that is going on is not for spheres of influence; it has to do with presence. The Americans and the Soviets, the British, the French, the various Arab nations, the Islamic factions, the Japanese, and gradually the Chinese are all establishing a presence in Oman, in Saudia Arabia, in Iran, and in Israel. The makeup of each of these items that I referred to as a presence is gradually affecting the balance of power in the area.

MR. SAUNDERS: I draw from your analysis a picture of a Western strategy that would combine the various Western presences as you describe them in this area so that their relationships with countries in the area would be the predominant set of relations and would, therefore, deny the Soviets a predominant position in the area. Is that a viable strategy—to put all one's eggs in the basket of a strategy like that?

MR. NEWSOM: Let me first comment on what Jim Critchfield said. Maybe because I have battle ribbons from the Baghdad Pact and from the North Yemen escapade, I feel that we lived under illusions that were fortunately never challenged through two decades of the 1950s and 1960s and into the 1970s. We thought we had a sphere of influence and a secure strategic arrangement in the nations of the northern tier. It was, of course, an arrangement that we never formally joined. Every year we used to meet and decide what the United States could do for the Baghdad Pact that would not cost us any money or advance our commitments. Each of the countries in the Baghdad Pact, except for Turkey, perhaps, joined the pact for regional reasons of its own. It is ironic that today, when we talk about a lesser position in the area, we have more military power in the area in the two carrier task forces in the Indian Ocean on a constant basis than we ever had during the period of the Baghdad Pact. We had certain intelligence access and certain political advantages, but we should not look back at that as a period in which the area was in any general sense secure. I am not sure, therefore, that it is correct to say that a sphere of influence existed, which has now disappeared.

When we analyze the Soviet motivations in the area, we also need to analyze very coolly the motivations of the nations in the area that are cooperating with us. We do not listen very carefully sometimes to what they are saying to us. What they seem to be saying to us sometimes is, Yes, there is a threat to us. We have not defined it very clearly. The United States is naturally moved by a Soviet threat, so we will talk about the Soviet and Communist threat. The U.S. relationship with us, they are saying, is an embarrassment. We want to continue it, but we want to justify it. The best way to justify it is for the United States to provide us with substantial military equipment, which can be done under a security rubric. They are also saying that they need to handle the politics of the area; even if we do not fully understand what they are doing, we must accept it. Thus, there is the very ambivalent Saudi attitude, for example, toward the regime in South Yemen and the very difficult episode that we went through in trying to help North Yemen through the Saudis. We have the Pakistanis wanting our military equipment, but wanting to remain nonaligned and probably looking still more apprehensively east than they do west. The deterrent to substantial Soviet military moves in the area has always been the threat of American reaction. That threat, in the presence of our fleet, is still there. We certainly want to cooperate closely with the countries in the area, because, for one thing, we want to keep them from being neutralized in a way that reduces our access. We should not, however, have illusions about the degree to which they will become realistically a part of a strategic framework.

MR. SAUNDERS: Let me pose a political problem. A lot of people say that the Soviets are moving; they are in Afghanistan, they are on their way to the Persian Gulf. That is a clearly defined threat that a lot of people can understand. Our response is that we are going to develop a Western presence in the area. We will have an economic presence and a political presence; we may even be able to do a little bit about the Arab-Israeli-Palestinian problems and enhance our diplomatic posture and our ability to influence events in the area. We are going to have a military force, part of which may be able to get to the area in one week, or in three weeks, or in five weeks. This is the way we will keep the Soviets out of an area that everyone agrees is absolutely vital to the Western alliance. I could say that; I probably have said it in congressional testimony. It is not, however, a very convincing or comfortable posture to be in. How can one define this as a policy that makes some kind of sense to the political leader who has to build a consensus around it?

MR. CRITCHFIELD: We lived for thirty years with a jerry-built, improvised, flawed world that we considered a safe security arrangement. The interesting thing is that it worked; nothing happened during these years, we did not lose anything significant. This era is gone. The new forward line of our position of influence is somewhere offshore, and the people in the area are happy to have it that way. They are delighted when they hear the kind of estimate that David Newsom just made, that we have twice the fire power we ever had. They think that is just marvelous, particularly because it is not quite here. They are living in a world in which they are hopeful that they can get through the next twenty years with the Soviets kept in the Soviet Union, and the Americans kept over the horizon, and the rest of them somehow muddling through. That is the real framework within which we have to attempt to formulate some kind of an American policy.

MR. SAUNDERS: Don't we have a situation now in which the illusions of the past will not work because Iran is not what it was three to twenty-five years ago, and the Persian Gulf is not what it was for the last decade? Afghanistan is no longer a buffer between the Soviets and Southwest Asia. There is, therefore, the potential for Soviet encroachments within this gray area. There is already, in some people's view, a threatening presence there that could alter the character of the area and shift it from being nonaligned to becoming some kind of new Soviet sphere of influence. How does one construct a credible policy to deal with that?

RICHARD BRODY, Pan Heuristics: The Persian Gulf is still in the same geographic position relative to the United States and the Soviet Union that it was twenty years ago. The military situation is not the same now as it was then, not because of the Central Treaty Organization (CENTO), which, as you say, was always a paper organization, but because of the Soviet capability to transport its forces there. That ability has changed tremendously since the 1950s because of improved airlift capability and because of new road structure on both sides of the border. In the 1950s, we had access to Turkey on a fairly free basis, as we showed in the Lebanon crisis. That is no longer true, as we witnessed in our attempts to use Turkey in some of the more recent Middle East crises. The dependence of the West on Middle Eastern oil was very different in the 1950s. Europe used Middle Eastern oil then, but the percentage of its total energy needs supplied by the Middle East was much lower. We were much better equipped to handle a contingency there than were the Soviets. There has been a trend in a certain direction; perhaps there can be a trend to reverse that direction.

MR. SAUNDERS: I would like someone to offer some ray of hope about a policy for where we are going and how to protect our interests while we get there.

GHASSAN BISHARA, *Elfajr* (Jerusalem newspaper): The consensus in the government seems to be that, in order to protect U.S. interests in the Middle East, militarily at least, there is a need to have the Rapid Deployment Force. There is a need for negotiations to have some countries there accept American bases for use with the Rapid Deployment Force. That may take some convincing, however, because many people in the region feel that the Soviet Union is not really an oppressor. The Soviet Union is not about to attack; it has not so far. Another country, Israel, is occupying part of the Arab world, and the United States is trying to convince the Arabs that the threat is not from Israel, but from the Soviet Union. Certainly it is in the U.S. interest to protect the Persian Gulf to ensure continued supplies of oil and to stop Soviet expansion into the region. If that is to be done militarily, which we all seem to agree, then there must be a moderation or a neutralization of Arab peoples' sentiments, which seem to be hostile to this U.S. thesis. Israel is very serious about keeping this gap between the Arab regimes and people and the West. In 1955 or 1956, the Israeli Mossad sent terrorists to Cairo when Nasser's new regime was about to reach some agreement with the Western powers, Britain in particular. These people placed bombs in Cairo movie theaters and British cultural offices. The intention is really to keep this gap between the West and the Arab people. Witness the tremendous opposition within the United States to supply Awacs to Saudia Arabia. Israel and U.S. policy makers are aware that the Saudis really will not use these Awacs against Israel, even against Israel's intention to conduct a preemptive attack. The Arab concern is to create friction between Israel and the United States by not allowing weapons to be sold, which would create more anti-American feelings in the region. The friction would result in keeping the United States to itself. The Middle East is our area; we want to deal with it.

MR. SAUNDERS: The situation is perhaps not so hopeless as I have deliberately painted it in order to provoke people. I do feel, however, that it is desirable to see whether we can articulate some sort of approach to this collection of problems. An active American policy across the area dealing with the Palestinian problem, attempting to cope with potential sources of conflict within the area, developing a substantial military presence in the area, contributing our very substantial economic weight, which does affect the course of events in the area—out of all of that, there is a posture, a presence, a set of relationships that could give us a strong position in the area vis-à-vis the Soviet Union. It is difficult to reduce that to a concise, understandable, politically salable policy in this country.

# 4

# The Arab-Israeli Peace Process: Supplying the Missing Ingredients

A CONVERSATION WITH HAROLD H. SAUNDERS

*July 21, 1981*

My purpose today is not, as I have had to do so many times in the past, to write the paper on the next step in moving the Arab-Israeli peace process forward. I want to step back from that for a moment and reduce the problem to its essentials in an effort to regain our bearings and to reestablish a sense of direction. I do this with deep respect for those who must work with other governments and peoples to move the process forward one day and one document at a time.

I am not going to rehearse background; I am not going to review reasons why moving toward an Arab-Israeli settlement is important to peace and to U.S. interests in this area; I am not going to offer my own prescription for a settlement. I simply want to lay out several touchstones for policy to get us back to basics. I want to remind us all of what needs to be added to the peace process if it is to move again. The exact formulas for putting together agreements must emerge from the exchanges among political leaders, but they will not come up with sound solutions unless they are addressing real issues.

I would only say for the sake of perspective that we are now at the end of the long months of the American and Israeli election campaigns when the process of Arab-Israeli negotiations can be resumed. The secretary of state has visited the Middle East to start developing common ground between the Reagan administration and friendly governments in the area. That trip will be followed with visits of their leaders to Washington for meetings with our president and other top leaders. Out of the preparations for these visits and out of the talks themselves should come some sense of what the steps in the peace process will be, how urgently they must be taken, and what their objective in the next chapter will be.

My message today, in short, is this: Progress toward resolution of the Arab-Israeli conflict depends now on engaging Israel's eastern neighbors in the peace process. Engaging Israel's eastern neighbors will spotlight the historic Israeli-Palestinian conflict. Negotiated resolution of the Palestinian problem in all its aspects requires a settlement that respects the desire of both Israelis and Palestinian Arabs for a homeland of their own in the former Palestine mandate. Because there is no common understanding among these parties, affirmation of the purpose and basis of negotiation is a prerequisite to progress as the new chapter of the peace process begins. Since the credibility of American power is at stake, the American position on what a just and secure peace requires must be clear.

### Reaffirming Basics

To start, I want to probe to the heart of what we call the peace process to isolate as precisely as possible the problems to be addressed in the next chapter of efforts to move the Arab-Israeli conflict toward resolution.

The first job in any negotiating process is to achieve agreement about the purpose of the negotiation and the shape of a solution that could come out of the negotiation. Until the parties to the negotiation are talking about the same general objective, the negotiation cannot go anywhere. Negotiation can bridge the gap between conflicting claims only when the parties are ready to find common ground among available compromises. When either party insists on an all-or-nothing settlement, the only solution is surrender and not a negotiated resolution. Determining whether two parties are ready to negotiate a solution to conflicting claims requires answering whether they agree that the time has come for a negotiated solution; answering that question in turn requires some understanding of the overall shape of a possible compromise.

In this case, there are two problems to be dealt with. One problem for several decades has been to define whether and, if so, how Jews and Arabs will live together in peace and mutual acceptance in the land geographically defined by the Palestine Mandate west of the Jordan River. Another way to put this is to say that one purpose of the next chapter in the negotiating process is to achieve peace between Israel and the Palestinian people. The second problem, which hinges on the first, is to define whether and, if so, how Israel will live at peace with neighboring states as an accepted and recognized state in the Middle East.

This is not an academic issue. Some Arabs and some Israelis do not yet agree that Arabs and Jews should live together at peace in

Palestine on the terms available. Some Arabs still do not accept that there should be a Jewish homeland there, and some Israelis today believe either that the land of Israel encompasses all of Palestine or at least that the establishment of a Palestinian homeland would jeopardize the security and boundaries of their own state. On the other hand, many Arabs today are prepared to live at peace with a Jewish state. Many Israelis acknowledge that peace with the Palestinian Arabs is essential and that there will be no peace while the Palestinian Arabs remain under military occupation. Serious negotiation is unlikely until there is agreement that the purpose is a negotiated peace between Israel and the Palestinian people.

This is an operational issue. Israel has refused to negotiate with the Palestine Liberation Organization in part because the PLO charter does not accept the existence of the Jewish state and because there is no authoritative, unequivocal, and convincing statement from the Palestinian movement on behalf of a majority of Palestinians that they are prepared to live at peace with Israel. I hasten to add that Israeli authorities also say they will not talk to the PLO because of its terrorist actions. The question is what Israeli policy would be if there were an unequivocal statement of readiness to make peace on behalf of the Palestinians and to do so only by peaceful means. We have to remember that President Sadat's visit to Jerusalem broke an impasse in the peace process not because he made substantive concessions in his speech to the Knesset—he did not—but because his presence before the Knesset dramatized concretely and convincingly Egypt's acceptance of Israel and its readiness to make peace and normalize relations with it.

Some Palestinians refuse to provide the recognition of Israel that could give the peace process a new lease on life because they feel there is no unequivocal and convincing Israeli statement recognizing their right to a homeland of their own alongside Israel. They have refused to enter negotiations under the Camp David framework in part because they believe Israeli actions in occupied territories are evidence that Israel does not intend to negotiate in good faith toward the establishment of a Palestinian Arab homeland. They are convinced that the Israeli government requires an all-or-nothing solution rather than a negotiated settlement.

A critical question in determining whether a negotiated solution is possible is establishing a common view of the shape a negotiated solution might take. In this case, the question is: What will the terms of the peace be? Many Arabs say that they will make peace so long as it is a just peace and not unconditional surrender. Most Israelis want peace but cannot accept a peace that does not provide long-term assurance of security for the state of Israel. Many of them say they see the existence of a Palestinian homeland as a threat to Israel's security.

Over the years three possible solutions have been proposed as the basic terms for peace between these two peoples asserting claims to the same land. The first is for all of them to live together in one unified secular state. This would mean that there would be no Jewish and no Arab state in Palestine, but a state of Palestine in which all residents would live together with guarantees for their individual, religious and ethnic rights. The arguments for this approach, at best, have been based on the belief that a state is possible in which people of different backgrounds can live and work together in harmony. The arguments against it are rooted in the Jewish experience that they cannot count on living without discrimination and persecution outside a Jewish state.

A second approach has been to divide the land between them. The members of the United Nations in 1947 voted support for this solution when they approved partitioning the land, and a Jewish state has been established and accepted to membership in the United Nations. The issue was posed again in 1967 in UN Security Council Resolution 242: In a context of Israeli withdrawal from occupied territories and the establishment of secure and recognized boundaries, there will be peace between Israel and its neighbors. To this day, however, there has not been agreement on this solution.

A third approach has been to try to define a process through which Israelis and Palestinians could seek some kind of relationship in the West Bank and Gaza that would allow Palestinian Arabs political self-expression while allowing Israel some presence for the preservation of its security and for fulfilling what Israelis feel is their right to live in the historic land of Israel. This was the approach articulated at Camp David in the concept of autonomy for the Palestinians in the West Bank and Gaza through a transitional period until a negotiation with full Palestinian participation could determine the final status of these territories. Meanwhile, the parties could test their ability to live side by side at peace. The feasibility of this approach depends on the conviction of each side that the ultimate solution to emerge from the process can fulfill its legitimate objectives.

The issue is simply: *If* Jews and Arabs will live together at peace in Palestine, *how* will they live together? The world community has expressed its view that division of the land into two separate homelands is the most workable solution. Neither Israelis nor Palestinians

80

are unanimous in accepting that basic description of the shape of a solution.

Again, the point is an operational one. Because there is no agreement on the shape of a solution, negotiations on how to get there are stymied by hidden agendas on which each party holds its real objectives without declaring them. One reason that Arabs have no faith in the Camp David concept of autonomy for the Palestinian Arabs in the West Bank and Gaza through a transitional period is their conviction that Israel's hidden agenda includes the exercise of Israeli sovereignty in those territories. One reason the Israelis fear negotiations that might lead to an independent Palestinian state is their fear that the Palestinians' hidden agenda includes the ultimate establishment of one secular state in Palestine.

As the new chapter in the Arab-Israeli peace process opens and as the new U.S. administration develops its strategy toward the entire Middle East and Southwest Asia, serious attention must be given to ways of reaffirming the basis for peace negotiations.

I am not suggesting tying up the negotiating process—any more than it already is—until these issues are resolved, and I am not suggesting head-on confrontations over them.

I am suggesting that these issues should again be brought to a prominent place in discussions on strategy for advancing the peace process. To proceed without recognizing that today we do not have a common view of the purpose of the negotiation and the shape of a negotiated solution is to accept stalemate. To proceed while making efforts to reduce the hidden agendas may open doors to broadening the peace process.

While we do not want to tamper with already agreed bases for negotiation, we should not gloss over the fact that widening gaps between interpretations of existing statements raise questions about how sound a foundation for a renewed negotiating process now exists. Since most Middle Eastern parties recognize these gaps and many believe there is no agreed foundation for negotiation, reaffirmation of the basis for negotiation is a prerequisite to progress.

Finally, I am suggesting that, since the credibility of American power is at stake, the U.S. administration needs to be clear about what it is and is not prepared to support. It needs to make the U.S. position clear to other parties to the peace process, because today there is widespread misunderstanding of our objectives. There can be no consensus about common objectives and strategies between us and our friends unless we are clear about ours.

# Defining the Peace Process

If it is important to reaffirm the basis for the peace negotiations and to advance them, the next question is how to define the diplomatic and negotiating process through which the necessary agreements on principle and detail can be reached.

In the peace efforts since 1967, the peacemakers have moved back and forth between two general approaches. Neither one is inherently better; each may be appropriate at different stages of the peace process. But it is useful to look at each for the opportunities it may offer. One approach is to seek agreement first through mediation or negotiation on the principles that will govern a settlement and then to work out the detailed arrangements for implementing the basic agreement. Resolution 242 itself is a negotiated statement of the broad principles of a settlement.

The advantages of this approach are that it can give detailed negotiations credibility and break the stalemate that prevents them from beginning. It would also remove the hidden agendas from negotiation. For instance, in the present situation, many Arabs say they would support a long transitional period in the West Bank and Gaza if it were agreed that an act of self-determination would take place at a specified date. An autonomous Palestinian self-governing authority in the West Bank and Gaza might become a credible transitional arrangement if Arabs and Israelis agreed that it is not intended to be the long-term solution.

The disadvantages are that political bodies are sometimes not able to make decisions on large principles unless they know how they can be implemented and that principles implemented without details spelled out are subject to multiple interpretations. Again, Resolution 242 is the prime example of a statement of principles that has in the past fourteen years been so variously interpreted that one might say that it is accepted in name by the key parties and in fact by none. The Camp David framework is also subject to major differences in interpretation, even by those who negotiated it.

The second approach is the response to the weaknesses of the first. Its starting point is the premise that ultimate questions cannot be resolved head-on but only through a series of negotiations that serve as building blocks. Each is designed to produce an agreement that will allow each party to test the other's ability and willingness to carry out its terms as a basis for developing a peaceful relationship. The diplomacy of 1973–1975 through the Kissinger shuttles and, in a different way, the 1978 Camp David framework on a comprehensive peace were built on the judgment that neither side was ready to make the decisions required by an ultimate settlement but that partial or interim agreements could be reached that would accumulate over time. These would make decisions on a final settlement possible at some point. That is why the Camp David framework itself provided for negotiation in two stages.

The advantages of this approach are that it may be all the political traffic will bear in the participating countries at a given time and that it does provide constructive movement toward peace, which may make broader decisions possible later.

The disadvantage is that there may come a time in a negotiating process when partial agreements are no longer possible without some understanding about the principles of a larger settlement. We had reached that point between Egypt and Israel with the Sinai II agreement in 1975. It took a secret understanding on total Israeli withdrawal to the international boundary to set the stage for President Sadat's trip to Jerusalem, Camp David, and the peace treaty. Lack of an understanding on principles of an Israeli-Palestinian settlement since Camp David has been critical in the failure to win the support of the eastern Arabs for the Camp David framework.

As the new chapter in the peace process opens, there is a need again to find some combination of these approaches that fits the present situation. In approaching this decision, two points stand out. First, the future will be built on a past that, as a matter of reality, includes three interim agreements in 1974–1975, President Sadat's visit to Jerusalem, the Camp David accords, and the Egyptian-Israeli peace treaty. Not only can these achievements ratified by two parliaments not be erased; significant agreements were reached there that should not be lost, even though important issues were left unresolved.

The Camp David framework applying to the Palestinian issue put the Palestinian issue at the top of the negotiating agenda in the next round of the peace process. However the process proceeds, it will start from the fact that the Israeli Knesset has ratified a document that states, among other things, that negotiations are necessary for the purpose of carrying out all provisions and principles of Resolutions 242 and 338; that the objective is a just, comprehensive, and durable settlement of the Middle East conflict through the conclusion of peace treaties based on those resolutions in all their parts; that there should be negotiations on the resolution of the Palestinian problem in all its aspects; that arrangements emerging from these negotiations should give due consideration both to the principle of self-government by the inhabitants of the West Bank and Gaza and to the legitimate security concerns of the parties involved; that the negotiations shall be based on all the provisions and principles of UN Security Council Resolution 242; that the negotiations will resolve, among other matters, the location of boundaries and the nature of security arrangements; and that the resolution from the negotiations must also recognize the legitimate rights of the Palestinian people and their just requirements.

The concepts of the framework are rooted in political reality. They took account of an Israeli proposal for self-rule in the West Bank and Gaza and the need to develop it into a plan for full autonomy as a transition to a final settlement. Those concepts were also hammered out in negotiation. They provide a practical sequence of steps for elections, negotiations, self-government, and referenda. Their shortcomings lie not in the concepts but in the interpretation that has limited them since their negotiation.

Second, it is also a fact that President Sadat's visit to Jerusalem, the Camp David accords, and the Egyptian-Israeli peace treaty were based on agreement that the objective is a comprehensive peace, but the approach has not won the broader Arab support needed for a comprehensive peace. It is a truism that the peace process cannot lead to a comprehensive peace unless it engages the Arab parties on Israel's eastern borders. They will not engage unless they see a process unfolding that does not appear to be a cover for what they view as a steady program of de facto Israeli annexation of the West Bank and Gaza.

In operational terms, two choices have been put forward in defining the 1981–1982 edition of the peace process. One is to resume the talks between Egypt and Israel within the Camp David framework to establish an autonomous Palestinian regime in the West Bank and Gaza while attempting to win broader Arab support for that process. Another approach is to assume, as most of the rest of the world does, that any process going under the name "Camp David" has been so discredited that it cannot win broader Arab support and therefore start again to try to build a fresh base for some new negotiating process.

My own recommendation begins with two thoughts about the above analysis. First, to continue the autonomy talks alone, picking up only where they left off, will be to ignore the essential purpose of the peace process itself. That purpose is gradually to engage all the key parties to the Arab-Israeli conflict in the process of making peace and building normal relationships. Second, to scrap what has been achieved, on the other hand, would be to ignore political realities that are critical in producing the further decisions necessary to new steps in the peace process.

This analysis adds up, in my view, to continuing a building-block strategy starting with two key components. First, we must at an appropriate time discuss with Egypt and Israel the resumption of the autonomy talks. We must make clear our view that success will depend in part on eventually gaining broader Arab support. We must also make clear that we will participate only as long as a serious effort is made to reach agreement on the full autonomy we believe was agreed at Camp David. One demonstration of the seriousness of the negotiation will be an understanding that all issues, such as Israeli settlements, will be dealt with in the negotiation and will not be resolved unilaterally outside the negotiation.

Second, we must begin a serious dialogue with the key Arab parties on Israel's eastern front to begin a process of establishing a basis for negotiating peace between them and Israel. The objective would be negotiations among the parties, but I would not recommend at the outset attempting to determine a forum for such negotiations; the door could be left open initially for any form of exchange, direct or indirect, secret or open. I would also not recommend starting with the explicit purpose of persuading them to join or to support the autonomy talks. Two basic questions could be the starting point for the dialogue: On what basis would the Arabs make peace with Israel and support the establishment of an authority during Israeli withdrawal from the West Bank and Gaza and the establishment of security measures and the skeleton of Palestinian government? Peace cannot be achieved without the eventual participation of these parties, and cooperation against Soviet penetration cannot be strengthened to its maximum unless Egypt's alienation is ended and the United States is seen as champion of values and interests shared by the key Arab moderates. One Arab ambassador told me recently that the United States is increasingly seen as the enemy.

This approach would require a broad diplomatic effort closely related to resumption of the autonomy talks but reaching well beyond them in new exploratory probes to broaden the base for the peace process.

### Breaking the Impasse

To go beyond dialogue on Israel's eastern front, to break the present impasse, and to develop the groundwork for negotiation will require not only a readiness on our part to discuss the basic purpose of the negotiation and the shape of a solution with Israel and its eastern neighbors and an effort to do what we can to lead the autonomy talks to a serious transitional result. It will also require a concrete and undeniable demonstration that each party is ready to address the other party's basic concerns and to make peace—a demonstration that can break the psychological barriers of suspicion and distrust.

Any effort to break the psychological impasse must address these concerns. After centuries of cruel rejection and pain in reestablishing a Jewish homeland, the Israelis maintain that the heart of the Arab-Israeli conflict is Arab acceptance of Israel as a Jewish state in the Middle East. They believe that many Arabs are still committed to the destruction of Israel, and concrete evidence of Arab acceptance is the essential minimum for Israel. I remember a conversation with Prime Minister Golda Meir in which Egypt's closure of the Suez Canal was being discussed. What she spoke about was not the harm to Israel's interests. She said it made her think of the sign on a door in the Russian town where she grew up that warned, "No Jews." What was important to her was the symbol of nonacceptance. What President Sadat provided in his trip to Jerusalem was not a substantive breakthrough in the negotiations but convincing evidence that his government was prepared to accept Israel as a neighbor, to make peace with Israel, and to normalize relations. Many elements in the Arab position—including the Palestinian National Charter—are concrete symbols to the Israelis of nonacceptance and rejection.

The Arabs since the disintegration of the Ottoman Empire have sought the right to work out their own destiny in homelands of their own—the right of self-determination in the full meaning of the term. They have suffered foreign occupation in this area for centuries, most recently within the Turkish Empire. Many of them have seen the Zionist settlement of Palestine and the establishment of Israel as another form of Western colonization on land they regard as their own. Their understanding of historic agreements relating to the establishment of a Jewish homeland is that this would be achieved without prejudice to the Arab inhabitants of the land. Today they see Palestine divided and a Jewish state established, but they see nothing on the Arab side of the equation. The goal of those who accept division of the land between Arabs and Jews is to exercise the right of self-determination in an Arab portion of a partitioned Palestine. Any negotiating process that does not seem to them to recognize this right cannot succeed.

Perhaps this is a moment to walk into the minefield of self-determination. Americans should reflect long and hard on the fact that America's apparent rejection of the principle of self-determination is a major factor in the erosion of U.S. credibility as a major power in the Middle East. Americans should also reflect long and hard on the fact that any American official who applies the word publicly to resolution of the Arab-Israeli conflict is subjected to every abuse from verbal criticism to subtle character assassination.

Let's see if we cannot clear the air by making some objective observations. First, I know of no way to say that the United States does not fully endorse the principle of self-determination. The concept is rooted in principles put before the world in the Declaration of Independence. It reflects the ideals of self-government and consent of the governed written into our Constitution. It was brought to the councils of statesmen attempting to frame a world order in the twentieth century by the president of the United States. It is repeated again and again as a right of peoples in the United Nations Charter and in other key documents of the United Nations, to which the United States as well as Israel has subscribed. Reading Chapter I, Article I, paragraph 2 of the Charter, the purposes of the United Nations include this one: "To develop friendly relations among nations based on the principle of equal rights and self-determination of peoples and to take other appropriate measures to strengthen peace. . . ."

Second, the issue is not whether the United States is for or against the principle of equal rights and self-determination but how it is to be applied in a given situation in a way that protects the rights of all parties to the maximum extent possible. The formal position of the United States, described on numerous occasions at the United Nations, has two main points: (1) an independent state is not necessarily the only outcome of an act of self-determination; (2) there are many instruments through which an act of self-determination can take place, including consultation, mediation, negotiation, elections, and referenda. The issue in the present situation is not whether we must respect the principle of self-determination; the issue is to achieve agreement on a process that allows the exercise of that principle in a practical and politically feasible way.

Third, negotiations over how to give practical expression to the principles of equal rights and self-determination are today blocked by the fact that the word self-determination has now become one of those Mid-Eastern codewords meaning independent Palestinian state. The Israelis see an independent Palestinian state both as a symbol of the final partition of Palestine and as a state committed to the ultimate erosion of a separate Jewish state.

That point brings us full circle. The issue of whether the United States supports applying the principle of self-determination to resolution of the Israeli-Palestinian conflict is not the real issue. The real issue in breaking the psychological impasse is for the Israelis to assure the Palestinians—if they can—that Israel understands their basic desire to exercise the right of self-determination and for the Palestinians and other eastern Arabs that they accept Israel and are prepared to make peace and normalize relations with it and to exercise self-determination without jeopardizing Israel's security.

My third recommendation is that achieving a convincing demonstration by both sides of readiness to deal with basic concerns should be an early objective of American diplomacy in the new chapter of the peace process. It seems unlikely that negotiations can be joined with any Arab party on Israel's eastern borders until the Israelis are faced with a clear demonstration of Arab willingness to make peace and until the Israelis demonstrate convincingly that their objective is not continued expansion of Israel's borders by de facto annexation of the West Bank and Gaza.

If I were to express a specific hope in this context, it would be that the leaders of Jordan, Saudi Arabia, Syria, and the Palestinian movement would, after consultation among themselves, put themselves in a position to present a clear-cut statement of their readiness to make peace with Israel on conditions that they would spell out and that the leaders of Israel would find a way to make clear to those potential negotiating partners that they do not intend to absorb the West Bank through any means.

Achieving the clearest possible statements by both sides should be a high priority of those who are about to relaunch the peace process.

### Issues for Discussion

In light of the above analysis, there are certain decisions that the United States must make as it develops its strategy toward this problem. These might serve as a tentative agenda for our discussion. First, a key question is, Does the United States have an interest in the kind of resolution that is found for the Arab-Israeli conflict, or not? Does the United States remain committed to a solution of the problem as envisioned in resolution 242, or is the United States now prepared to acquiesce in the outcome of a continuing struggle between the two nationalisms with a claim to the land?

A second question is whether this is a critical moment, or not. How urgent is it to move firmly and vigorously over the next six to twelve months? Is there some point at which either the Israeli program of creating facts in the West Bank and Gaza will make a process of de facto exercise of sovereignty irreversible? On the other side, are the Arabs ready to make peace?

Third, how much should the United States invest in a major effort for moving toward a resolution of the conflict? An American effort firm enough and successful enough to be a demonstration of American diplomatic power will require the personal support and involvement of the president and the secretary of state along with a senior negotiator able to call on their support at any moment. This approach would require the president to outline American interests in this area and to explain to the American people why those interests require a settlement of this conflict in the near future. Among those interests would, of course, be our support for the long-term security of Israel.

Fourth, if a decision is made that the United States does have an interest in a just settlement, that the United States judges the near future to be a critical moment in the peace process, and that the United States is prepared to make a major effort, the operational decisions to be made are where to start putting together a diplomatic program that will build in the direction of a full-fledged effort.

## QUESTIONS AND ANSWERS

WILLIAM CRAWFORD, Islam's Centennial Fourteen: I am struck by the fact that nowhere in the discussion was there any mention of the Europeans. Would you be willing to comment on their possible involvement in this process?

MR. SAUNDERS: The criterion for the involvement of the Europeans and other major powers is that they be prepared to contribute to building a basis for the negotiation. The American position vis-à-vis Europe, at least at professional levels, has been that a contribution to building a basis for negotiation requires the Europeans to be in touch with both sides and to make an honest effort to build a basis from which both sides could join in negotiation. This is different from simply talking to one side of the conflict and spelling out the aspirations of one side. That continues to be my view. Europeans and Americans could profitably work in complementary ways. The decision that the Europeans have to make is whether or not they are prepared to engage in a genuinely complementary effort, being in touch as we are with both sides. To go one step farther, I would say that essentially the same criterion applies to the Soviet Union.

MR. CRAWFORD: Their interest and involvement offer a chance to a new American administration to get some fresh air into this problem, to get the United States off several hooks on which it has managed to impale itself over time. The responsibility should be spread around a bit; the more responsible involvement the better.

MR. SAUNDERS: The question is to what extent the Europeans are prepared to go down both sides to develop a basis for negotiation to which both sides can subscribe. Another question is how the Europeans can overcome the disadvantage they now have because they have not done that, that they are not at this point a credible interlocutor in Israel.

MR. BISHARA: Europe has access to both parties more than the United States does because the United States does not recognize or negotiate directly or indirectly with the Palestine Liberation Organization.

MR. SAUNDERS: I recognize the problem created by the fact that we are not in touch with the PLO. The United States still has potential credibility with the PLO precisely because it is the only power in touch with the Israelis. If the United States reached the point at which it could show sensitivity to the Palestinian side of the equation and a readiness to do something about it, that dialogue would take off on very short notice. The reverse is not true of the Europeans in approaching the Israelis.

MR. GREENE: I am more skeptical that the Reagan administration has the sense of urgency that you feel is required of an American political leadership to take on this kind of program of action, or even the basic decisions that are necessary to move it anywhere. This administration seems to have other priorities, both at home and abroad.

MR. SAUNDERS: I wonder if others would like to respond to that, just to round out a view on whether or not there will be an American sense of urgency to get on with the process.

MR. NEWSOM: The Reagan administration has come into office with the hope, if not with the conviction, that the attention of the states in the Middle East can be turned to what it considers the graver threat to the area, namely, the possibility of expanding Soviet influence. Recent events must cause many to think of them again, if not to come to different conclusions.

MR. SAUNDERS: It is not yet time to make a judgment as to what the

Reagan administration's policy toward this area is. The administration put domestic economic issues at the top of its priority list. It has sought time on the international front until the domestic economic package could pass through the necessary congressional route. As David Newsom said, events in the Middle East are now forcing its attention. Another set of important events will require the administration to think very hard about these issues—the series of visits that begin with President Sadat, then Israeli Prime Minister Begin, the Crown Prince of Saudi Arabia presumably, and the King of Jordan.

HELMUT SONNENFELDT, Brookings Institution: This issue of whether the present administration has a sufficient sense of urgency will settle itself, partly because events are imposing themselves and visits are scheduled. It is difficult to see how those visits can be conducted without talking about the issues of the Arab-Israeli conflict and the so-called peace process. I cannot tell from your discussion who you think the parties are. Would you enlighten me?

MR. SAUNDERS: The first two parties, of course, are those who have made peace with Israel, or made peace with each other—Egypt and Israel. When I talk about Israel's eastern neighbors joining the process, I am talking about two states bordering Israel—namely, Jordan and Syria, perhaps the first earlier than the second. I am talking about a third state, not as a party to the negotiation, but because the first two will require some sort of support from Saudi Arabia. Finally, I am talking about the Palestinians without attempting to define exactly how they will participate in the process. Of course, Camp David provided the opportunity for one million Palestinians to sit at or to be represented at the negotiating table. The issue is whether or in what way the PLO might join the process. I do not foresee that in the immediate future, but in my remarks I tried to leave the door open to any participant who is willing to declare a readiness to make peace with Israel. Do you want to elaborate on that?

MR. SONNENFELDT: I do not want to be contentious, but for someone who has no responsibility to leave doors open not to define the parties to the negotiation is one thing. For an administration that has to commit itself on these matters and that has to take the heat and the consequences of delay in making that kind of decision and then be charged with a lack of urgency, it seems to me is an incongruence in the discussion. At least a private individual ought to be able to say who he thinks the parties are and if he can impose that notion of who the parties are on the parties.

MR. SAUNDERS: I am enough of a practitioner still to feel that the key element in this process is to involve Palestinian representatives in whatever way is politically feasible and, in fact, in whatever way represents the Palestinian view. We have one approach to that. The Palestinians in the West Bank and Gaza are a party to the peace process by an agreement ratified by the parliaments of Egypt and Israel. That much is done. The next question is how one addresses the Palestinians outside that West Bank and Gaza. I leave that open at the moment, because what is going to happen first is that there will be a dialogue involving in some form Saudia Arabia, Jordan, Syria, and the PLO. Palestinian points of view may well be reflected in the first instance through the participation in some kind of process by those states. I do not want to go so far as to say that if the PLO were to declare its readiness to make peace with Israel on terms that seem sensible to everyone, the PLO still would not be party to the negotiation at some point down the line. Perhaps we must technically distinguish between the word "parties," which we all think of as formal representatives at the negotiating table, and participants in the process, some of them indirect, some of them direct.

ALTON FRYE, Council on Foreign Relations: We began the question period with what may be the central focus that would be serviceable for the near term. You asked what would be the timeliness or usefulness of an American initiative at this stage. It may be that an American initiative, despite the troubling events at this juncture, is not timely. There may well be a kind of interaction between an unfolding European role and an unfolding European effort to get into the act, even if it cannot meet the desirable criterion of having effective access evenhandedly to both the Israelis and the Arabs. There have been developments in Israeli politics that would lead an outside observer to wonder whether any substantial movement can take place from that side until further developments have occurred in Israeli politics. Those developments might be influenced for good or for ill by the sense that the United States, as the principal external friend, is coming under great pressure from other friends of the United States. They might be influenced by the perception that the Reagan administration may have to make choices between the alliance relationships central to its security and its close ties with Israel historically. Those kinds of more complicated and more subtle interactions could lead to a situation in which the role for the European initiative is not direct at all but might enhance the capacity of the United States to deal more constructively when it resumes its activity. We may have to go through a period while that effort plays out before there would be a timely opportunity for the United States.

MICHAEL NEIDITCH, staff of Congressman Benjamin S. Rosenthal: We ought to look very closely at the opportunities that may arise for us from a European initiative, and we may sadly have to dismiss them because of their unacceptability in Jerusalem. Lord Carrington is not acceptable. French President François Mitterand more than likely would be, but to sit and wait while the Europeans sort themselves out takes too much time. I also fear that Washington is not about to give up its prime place to the Europeans. With the present Israeli government in power, movement is not likely from that quarter, so perhaps we have to turn to the Arab world and hope that the very group that we find so difficult to mention by name, the PLO, seizes the initiative and presents in its own way an opportunity in a moment similar to President Sadat's in November of 1977. Perhaps the PLO will find it possible, given its own factions, to offer conditional recognition of Israel in return for an Israeli willingness to negotiate. If this administration is reluctant to seize the initiative, if the Europeans are not in a position to move it forward, and if the Israelis are unwilling to do so, the burden seems to fall on the Arab world. I sense that we may be close to a moment when the PLO may find it possible to say, "If you are willing to talk about the legitimacy of Palestinian nationalism, we are prepared to talk about the recognition and security of the state of Israel."

MR. SAUNDERS: It does impose a substantial burden on the Arab side. Whenever I have spoken to Arab friends about the possibility of a clear statement of position on the Eastern Arab front, I have gotten back the question why they should do this before the Israelis recognize their nationalism.

AMBASSADOR BASHEER: If Yasser Arafat turns out to be a Ghandi and declares that he is willing to recognize, in the territory of June 1, 1967, the right of Israel to exist, to accept a transitional period in which the West Bank and Gaza will not be militarized, what will the United States do if Israel answers no, as it did in its election, in its parties, in its official stand? This scenario is attractive, but it rests on the assumption that each party is willing to recognize the other, and that assumption has been elusive. We are talking about a problem completely different from its reality. The reality is that for a

93

number of years the Arabs refused to accept Israel. Then the Arabs moderated to accept Israel within a given border. Then Israel refused to accept the reality of the Palestinians, aside from people living under Israeli sovereignty. That is the problem. If the PLO accepts an act of superhuman sacrifice and Israel says no, what would happen? If Arafat today accepts a request to speak to the Knesset, how will he be received there, with roses or bullets?

MR. SAUNDERS: This is why I raised the question in slightly elliptical terms. We negotiated Resolution 242 almost fourteen years ago. Does the United States have a stake in that kind of solution, or are we prepared now to acquiesce in a solution that would result from a contest of power between the two rival nationalisms? I would like to hear you comment on what the interest of the United States is between those two choices.

JOSEPH EGGER, writer: I would like to break down the interest of the United States to the American Jewish community. In today's *New York Times*, there were several letters. A letter from three rabbis, one president of the World Council of Synagogues, another president of the Rabbinical Assembly, another executive vice-president of the Union of American Hebrew Congregations, and another letter by the vice-president of the Union of American Hebrew Congregations. That is four rabbis in today's *Times*. A week or two ago, there was a piece on the op-ed page of the *Times* by Rabbi Hertzberg. Not too long before that, there was a letter by the president of the Conference of Presidents of Major Jewish Organizations. That is at least five front-line, powerful, American-Jewish leaders. In each of these letters, there is an indication of a break in the monolithic, unquestioning support for recent and current Israeli government policy and actions. I would like to turn to the other side for just a moment. I have been doing some research on the PLO and statements from the PLO. I find quite a few statements of willingness to accept the state of Israel, and I have ocumentation. For quite a long while, there were virtually no statements in the American-Jewish community that were counter to the policies of the Israeli government for reasons of fear and security, very solid reasons on the part of the Jewish community in Israel and the Diaspora. Now there seems to be a clear break in that. The question remains, How does that get broken? It gets broken by talk, by discourse between the parties involved. The parties involved are the PLO, the only representatives of the Palestinian people, and the Israelis. The only party with sufficient power to get this stalemate off center is the U.S. government. The time seems to be now. With the break on the part of leaders in the American-Jewish community, what is needed is some support, some initiative from the American government, which is, of course, a determining factor in the existence of Israel, to bring together the parties.

MR. SAUNDERS: The president of the United States could spell out American interests in the Middle East, including, of course, the commitment to the state of Israel, in a way that would in no way jeopardize that security. He could do that in a way that would not offend members of the American-Jewish community. I have written a half dozen of those speeches, if not more, over my years in the government, and I have seen them again and again turned aside because of fear that for some reason it would be politically disadvantageous for political leadership in this country to make such a statement. Such a statement need not be confrontational with anyone. Indeed, its purpose should be to enlist the cooperation of all in the process. If that were done, we would have a base from which dialogue could break loose. Even though dialogue with the Palestinians might be unpopular in certain quarters, if it were conducted within the context of a commitment to peace with Israel, at least it would be justifiable and defensible in many quarters. It is essential for us, as the United States, at this point to know and say what we believe about the basics of a negotiating process. This responds in part to what Tahseen Basheer said. It could be done; others in this country would have every right to debate whether or not there was agreement with such a statement. I have been encouraging the need for a national consensus, some broad bipartisan base for the conduct of policy in the Middle East. That cannot happen unless somebody is willing to speak out about what our interests are and have a debate, as is going on within the Jewish community. That debate should take place in the Congress and other communities in the United States.

MR. CRAWFORD: I could not agree with you more about the need for a definition by leadership of true American interests in the situation. We tend to run scared of our own shadows in this country. In the Spring issue of the *Middle East Journal* is an opinion survey that is relevant to this problem. It shows that Palestinians, Arabs, and Iranians in general rank in public opinion about with the Japanese in the middle of the Second World War, but 90 percent of the Americans polled said the Palestinians must be involved in negotiation. That should give satisfaction and some courage to any leader to talk forthrightly about this problem.

MR. SAUNDERS: Would anybody like to hazard a guess as to why it is so difficult to launch this dialogue with the Palestinians in light of feelings expressed in such a public opinion poll?

HOWARD PENNIMAN, American Enterprise Institute: The answer to that is fairly simple in American terms. Political leaders, whether in Congress or in the White House, are concerned not about the general support that there might be for it, but about the specific opposition that might exist for each position. The fact that in general 90 percent approve does not say much of anything about how people will react in a specific electoral situation. The fact that there are some people who hold very strong views and continue to hold them within a segment of the community is something that is enough to worry almost any American politician. Unless there is a very severe crisis in which all persons can see that the solution to that crisis is one in which we must be united, we will continue to have an absence of dialogue, however wise it might be to follow your proposal. I do not want to criticize the proposal in any way; as a practical matter, however, it is highly unlikely that we will come to that point for at least the foreseeable future.

DAN PATTIR, American Enterprise Institute: I infer from your remarks that you have some kind of second thoughts or maybe some regrets about the outcome of Camp David and the peace treaty.

MR. SAUNDERS: I am not disappointed in any way about what we achieved at Camp David.

MR. PATTIR: I am speaking of Camp David not as a historical matter, but as a practical vehicle to continue what started in 1978 and 1979.

MR. SAUNDERS: I am disappointed in half of what has happened since Camp David. Of course I am not disappointed in the other half, which was the Egyptian-Israeli peace treaty. Those were important achievements, and I am proud of them. We should take a lot of credit for the autonomy talks because a lot of good work has been done. That will show up at some point in the process down the road. I am disappointed that we all—Egypt, Israel, and the United States—failed to win the support of Israel's eastern Arab neighbors for the Palestinian portion of what came out of Camp David. That is a disappointment; it should be a disappointment to all three parties to Camp David. That is the deficiency that we need to rectify at this point. We all recognize that it is a deficiency. It is not an issue between Israel and the United States or Egypt and Israel. The Arabs on the eastern side do not support Camp David; that is a fact with which we must cope. There will not be an agreement on Israel's eastern front until the other Arabs there do support some kind of peace process.

Notice that I carefully did not recommend leaving Camp David behind. I specifically recommend resuming the Camp David effort, but seeing through a separate effort whether or not we can build an environment that, at some point, will produce a track that can intersect with whatever we may gain out of the Camp David process. It is a rather subtle approach, but if we just go on with Camp David and do nothing on the eastern front beyond Camp David, we will have nothing in the end, even if we achieve the kind of agreement that might have come out of the negotiations of the past two years. I favor keeping all relevant courses in play, but trying to rejuvenate the one that we tried desperately to bring to fruition right after Camp David, when we made a great effort to persuade the Saudis and the Jordanians to relate to the process.

MR. PATTIR: Should we continue to rely on such vehicles as the Europeans or the rejectionist front to cooperate on a peace process, or should we abandon the vehicles that have been used so far?

MR. SAUNDERS: I certainly do not favor abandoning the vehicle; European credibility will not in the end be enhanced by simply rejecting Camp David. Camp David is a fact of life. It produced a peace treaty. It also put the Palestinian-Israeli conflict at the top of the negotiating agenda. Nobody should want to reject all that, so even where the Europeans are intelligently involved, they are working on the same problems that we were at Camp David. The representative of the European community has been addressing exactly the kinds of questions we have been addressing in the autonomy talks. The problem is there to be resolved. The problem is going to be the same whether it is defined by the Europeans, the Americans, the Egyptians, the Israelis, or the PLO. There are certain practical things that need to be done to resolve the problem, so I certainly would not subscribe to a European initiative because the Europeans have enhanced their credibility by rejecting Camp David. I would be intrigued by a European initiative based on a realistic recognition of the problems to be solved and a recognition that feasible solutions depend on participation of all parties, including, of course, the government of Israel.

MR. THIMMESCH: If President Reagan did make this statement about U.S. national interest in the Middle East, what kind of response would you anticipate from Prime Minister Begin?

MR. SAUNDERS: After long years of experience, I would be the last one to try to project in front of the press any sense of what Prime Minister Begin might do in response to an American initiative. If we are to continue the kind of close relationship with Israel that we have had in the past, we must put back together some kind of understanding of what our separate objectives are. In speaking of separate objectives, I do not speak of something that I regard as wrong. Israel is a sovereign nation with its own place in the world, its own tragic and unique history. It will, of course, have its own perspectives. The United States is a global power, and it will have its own perspectives as well. There is no reason why two nations like that cannot collaborate closely, but the collaboration must be based on a clear understanding of common interests. It is nothing more than an analytical statement to say that today we are not operating on the basis of similar perceptions of the other's interests. The actions taken by the government of Israel in recent days do not reflect America's view of what the peace process requires, what American interests require, what Israeli security and long-term prosperity require. We may be wrong. Israel may be right, but we need to talk that through. Until that has been done, and until common ground between us has been established, I find it difficult to see how our collaboration can move ahead fruitfully. If the president of the United States were to state American interests, it would be a great mistake if that were not accompanied by dialogue with Israel—in advance if desirable—in a way that could enhance the relationship between the countries. I am not in any way a subscriber to the notion that we ought to create a confrontation with the state of Israel. That will serve nobody's interests at all in this circumstance. Therefore, the art is to find a way to conduct that dialogue. It may very well be that the dialogue will not be very pleasant when we raise basic issues on which we have disagreed in the past. There has often been a period of crisis of confidence between the United States and Israel. That just has to be worked through, but friends do each other the worst disservice in human relationships if they do not make clear what will be the limits of their relationship with the other.

WALTER BERNS, American Enterprise Institute: I was somewhat puzzled by your statement about self-determination in the Middle East. If self-determination has any validity at all, it has its validity as it is expressed in the Declaration of Independence. There it takes the form that men are born with rights, natural rights. One of those rights is the right not to be governed without consent. To secure these rights, governments are instituted among men deriving their just powers from the consent of the governed. There is a disposition on the part of many Americans, far beyond what might be described as an Israeli lobby or a Jewish lobby, to recognize the fact that there is only one state in the Middle East that Thomas Jefferson would say recognizes this right to self-determination. Translated, many Americans believe that the Israelis have instituted a kind of government that we find familiar. Any discussion of the peace process that will involve the United States must take that into awareness. Israel is not simply a democracy; it is a democracy based, in a way, on a constitution—although it lacks one in fact—that recognizes the natural right not to be governed without one's consent. It is the only state in the area where that exists. That is important for us.

MR. SAUNDERS: There is no question that the existence of Israeli democracy is important to us. I would have to think about what the right of self-determination means in cultures where Western democracy is not the natural form of government. Other states in the Middle East have attempted parliamentary democracy and found it not consistent with their traditional ways of operating. There are systems for building the tribal base for government and tribal support for authority. These reflect a different kind of genius, which I do not pretend to understand. In a state like Saudi Arabia, however, there are efforts going forward today to try to figure out how that genius for representative government in some form can be translated into institutions in a modern state. Perhaps we do not want to presume that those nations have the right of self-determination only when they are going to subscribe in some way to a definition of democracy made in Washington or in Western Europe. Most of the world is not governed that way. Several dozen acts of self-determination have taken place under the United Nations Charter since 1948. All kinds of processes have been used with the understanding that these constitute acts of self-determination, processes for determining the will of the people. Some of them have simply been consultations among notables; others have involved more classic forms, such as elections. We cannot say that the right of self-determination only applies to those countries where the Western brand of democracy is practiced.

MR. BERNS: Much of what you said I would not disagree with. I only made my point in an effort to account for what seems to be an American attitude toward the problem there. That is self-determination as we have been taught to understand this subject and not without reason.

AMBASSADOR BASHEER: Professor Berns's concept of self-determination contradicts American independence. Britain was a very democratic country when it ruled over the colonies in North America, and yet the American people refused the British concept at the time of self-determination for independence. They fought a revolution against it.

Israel is a new country, thirty years old. Many of the people came from Palestine. They are adopting a Western technique, favored by you and many people, which is fine, but that should not deny the right of people who have other definitions of democracy to practice their own evolution like the Americans and other people who have evolved responsible governments.

Do people who practice any kind of system that you like have the right to annex and subjugate people that practice other systems? Can the Americans, because the Americans are democratic, rule over other countries in Latin America? Can any democracy colonize other countries on the advocacy that they are promoting self-determination? We were under British rule, and the British failed ever to give us self-determination. We had to fight for it. We should distinguish between colonizing the territories of other people by force and the right within our own community to practice whatever democracy we define. These are two different categories.

PROFESSOR SHARABI: Your excellent remarks, the operational and the practical, are a bit oriented toward a political context that no longer exists. In the summer of 1977, your remarks would still have been most relevant. The context then was the Brookings Institution Report, the Geneva Conference, the acceptance of the various parties of certain sets of principles for settlement. Now all this has changed. Let me point out two or three aspects of the context against which you are making your remarks now. In Israel, there is today a government that is not only ultrachauvinist, ultraorthodox in many of its members, but it is supported by a popular movement demonstrated in the recent election to have a vast consensus in Israel for its policies and objectives. The annexation of the West Bank, Gaza, and Arab Jerusalem puts the Begin or any other government in an inflexible position to negotiate beyond certain set parameters, those that would have to involve partial withdrawal, that would have to involve partition of the West Bank and Gaza. On the other side, the situation in the Arab world is quite dissimilar from that of four years ago. The situation derives from what they see happening in Israel itself and what they see happening in the United States. The credibility of the United States, of this administration, has suffered to the extent that governments that are moderate or friendly to the United States are themselves today in very difficult positions. Even the elements of moderation within the Arab governments and within the Palestinian movements are now on the defensive and might very soon be in retreat.

You raised a number of questions addressed to the administration itself. The question is whether the United States seeks to settle the Arab-Israeli problem, whether it sees any settlement of the Arab-Israeli conflict as a legitimate objective that should be pursued with energy, whether the area is subject to threats other than those that come from the Soviet Union. All these questions from the point of view of the government are answered not only in words but also in actions or nonactions. For the Palestinians and for the Arabs, the hesitation, the nonaction, the reflection of this administration does present a certain orientation of policy. They see it increasingly as coinciding with what is happening in Israel, as a consensus that is rejected in the area.

MR. SAUNDERS: This is one of the reasons, of course, why it is important that the administration clearly state its position on elements of the situation and on elements of a possible peace settlement.

Ms. KIPPER: We all owe Harold Saunders our thanks for the tremendous efforts he has made in preparing these meetings. Thank you.

# Selected AEI Publications

## AEI Associates Program